TWO-HOUR QUILTED CHRISTMAS PROJECTS

TWO-HOUR
QUILTED
CHRISTMAS
PROJECTS

Cheri
Saffiote

Sterling Publishing Co., Inc. New York
A Sterling / Chapelle Book

Chapelle:
- Jo Packham, Owner
- Cathy Sexton, Editor
- Staff: Malissa Boatwright, Kass Burchett, Rebecca Christensen, Marilyn Goff, Michael Hannah, Shirley Heslop, Holly Hollingsworth, Susan Jorgensen, Susan Laws, Ginger Mikkelsen, Barbara Milburn, Linda Orton, Karmen Quinney, Leslie Ridenour, Cindy Rooks, and Cindy Stoeckl

Artwork:
- Pauline Locke, Artist for Chapelle

Photography:
- Kevin Dilley, Photographer for Hazen Photography
- Susan Laws, Photo Stylist for Chapelle

If you have any questions or comments or would like information on specialty products featured in this book, please contact Chapelle, Ltd., Inc., P.O. Box 9252, Ogden, UT 84409 • (801) 621-2777 • (801) 621-2788 Fax

Library of Congress Cataloging-in-Publication Data

Saffiote, Cheri.
    Two-hour quilted Christmas projects / Cheri Saffiote.
        p.   cm.
    "A Sterling / Chapelle book."
    Includes Index.
    ISBN 0-8069-9771-0
    1. Christmas decorations.   2. Patchwork.   I. Title.
TT900.C4S18   1997
746.46'041 dc21   97-13978
                                            CIP

A Sterling/Chapelle Book

10 9 8 7 6 5 4 3 2 1

First paperback edition published in 1999 by
Sterling Publishing Company, Inc.
387 Park Avenue South, New York, N.Y. 10016
Produced by Chapelle Ltd.
P.O. Box 9252, Newgate Station, Ogden, Utah 84409
© 1997 by Chapelle Ltd.
Distributed in Canada by Sterling Publishing
c/o Canadian Manda Group, One Atlantic Avenue, Suite 105
Toronto, Ontario, Canada M6K 3E7
Distributed in Great Britain and Europe by Cassell PLC
Wellington House, 125 Strand, London WC2R 0BB, England
Distributed in Australia by Capricorn Link (Australia) Pty Ltd.
P.O. Box 6651, Baulkham Hills, Business Centre, NSW 2153, Australia
Printed in Hong Kong

Sterling ISBN 0-8069-9771-0 Trade
                0-8069-9772-9 Paper

ABOUT THE AUTHOR

Cheri's love of art began during her high school years as she excelled in all of her arts and crafts classes.

Shortly after high school, she married and today has four children. Throughout her child rearing years she has continued to do what she loves most — painting and sewing.

In 1988 she decided to make a business out of her hobby and Calico Station, a quilt and tole painting store, was opened. In what seemed to be an overnight success, she revolutionized the industry with her primitive designs and within the year she began publishing her work.

For the next three years she continued to be blessed with success and her store tripled in size. Calico Station Distribution, a distribution center for her published work, was opened and today her books, patterns, and kits are available through her distribution center as well as through retail stores nationwide.

Keep Your

CONTENTS

GENERAL INSTRUCTIONS

GATHERING SUPPLIES

Following is a list of general supplies that will be needed to make the projects in this publication. Other supplies, such as craft glue for gluing steps and fabric stiffener for making ornaments, may be needed for individual projects. In those instances, the additional supplies will be listed under the project's list of materials.

- Sewing machine
- Coordinating fabrics
- Pattern
- Pencil
- Fusible web
- Iron and ironing board
- Coordinating fabric scraps
- Fabric scissors
- Fade-away pen
- Fine-point permanent marker
- Cotton batting
- Needles
- Embroidery floss, coordinating color(s)
- Backing fabrics
- Pearl cotton
- Mismatched buttons

HOW TO: STEP ONE

Cotton fabrics have been used for the projects in this publication because they launder nicely, but when it comes to choosing fabrics, as long as types of fabrics are not mixed — anything goes!

Once all the coordinating fabrics have been cut into appropriate sized blocks, as designated in the list of materials for each project (height x width), they will be ready to be sewn together.

Using a $1/4$" seam allowance, machine-stitch fabric blocks together as shown in corresponding diagrams and/or photographs.

When piecing fabric blocks together to make quilt, pillow, or ornament fronts, first machine-stitch fabric blocks together in horizontal rows and press seams. Then stitch all horizontal rows together and press seams again.

Set pieced quilt, pillow, or ornament front aside.

HOW TO: STEP TWO

First, determine which direction the motif(s) should face. Any of the patterns in this publication can be "flipped" so they face the opposite direction. When using letters, they must be traced in reverse so they read correctly once they have been fused.

Lay the fusible web on top of the pattern(s) and trace the outer lines with a pencil.

If preferred, photocopy the pattern page(s), cut out the pattern(s), lay them on the fusible web, and trace.

Use a fade-away pen to transfer stitching lines for designs or letters onto fabric blocks. However, be careful when transferring onto tea-dyed muslin, the fade-away pen doesn't always disappear completely.

If desired, do the lettering freehand to add personalization.

HOW TO:
STEP THREE

Once the patterns have been transferred onto the fusible web, it is time to apply the fusible web onto fabric scraps that have been chosen for the motif(s).

Iron the fusible web onto the "back sides" of fabric scraps following manufacturer's instructions. Be certain the entire area of all patterns is fused.

Once fused, cut out designs, using fabric scissors, so edges are clean.

HOW TO: STEP FOUR

Using the designs that have been cut from fabric scraps, it is time to adhere them onto the quilt, pillow, or ornament front.

Remove the backing from the fusible web and iron the designs, following manufacturer's instructions, in position as shown in the corresponding photographs.

HOW TO: STEP FIVE

This step will provide the project with its "quilted" element.

Begin by placing the embellished quilt, pillow, or ornament front on top of the cotton batting.

Each of the designs, as specified in the individual projects, will be outlined with decorative stitches. See Glossary of Decorative Stitches on page 22.

Stitch by hand or with a buttonhole stitch on a sewing machine. In either case, be certain all stitching is done through both layers: the embellished front and the cotton batting.

Assembly instructions for each project specify two or three strands of embroidery floss for outlining the designs.

If preferred, use a single strand of quilting thread.

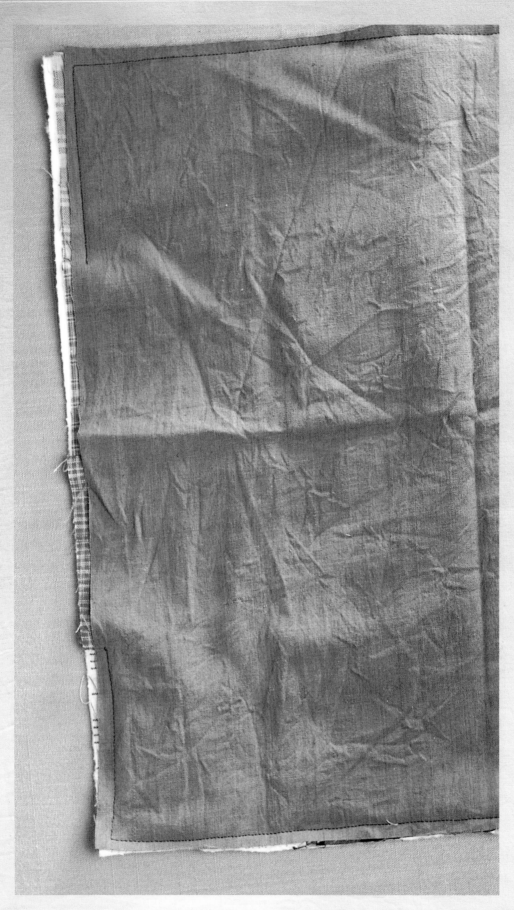

HOW TO:
STEP SIX

To finish the quilt, pillow, or ornament, the backing fabric must be machine-stitched to the quilted front.

With right sides together, machine-stitch around outside edges using a $\frac{1}{4}$" seam allowance.

Be certain to leave an opening for turning. It does not matter where the opening is; its random placement will add to the look of the finished piece.

It is not necessary to trim seams or clip corners.

HOW TO: STEP SEVEN

Once the quilt, pillow, or ornament has been finished with a backing fabric, turn it right side out.

If the open area is too small to place a hand into, use a ruler or the eraser-end of a pencil to shape all corners.

If making a pillow, stuff it to its desired fullness with polyester stuffing.

Whip-stitch with two strands of embroidery floss to close the opening.

If preferred, use a single strand of quilting thread.

HOW TO: STEP EIGHT

Some of the projects in this publication use hand- or machine-quilting as the final step.

This quilting step will add to the look of the piece and give the overall appearance of a unique, hand-made quilt, pillow, or ornament. However, this step can some-times be time consum-ing and may result in the project taking longer than two hours to complete. There-fore, it is offered only as an option and can be added to or deleted from any of the projects in this publication.

For the beginner, use a fade-away pen to draw the design(s) onto the finished quilt, pillow, or ornament front so that stitching is easier. For the experienced, stitch freehand, adding to the individuality of the finished piece.

HOW TO:
STEP NINE

Buttons can be the finishing touch to any quilt, pillow, or ornament and can be added to or deleted from any of the projects in this publication.

Using a needle with a large eye and pearl cotton, stitch the button(s) onto the project, generally going through all layers. Tie a knot in the pearl cotton to secure the button(s) and trim the ends.

Buttons make great "eyes" for motifs such as cats and snowmen, but stitched eyes can be used in place of buttons or, if desired, omit eyes.

If preferred, use matching buttons, but mismatched buttons give a unique, one-of-a-kind look to your "masterpiece!"

PIECING FABRIC BLOCKS, BORDERS & BACKS

PIECING FABRICS

The projects in this publication were created with the idea that they could be completed within two hours. Of course, that time is actual assembly time, and does not include time spent shopping for materials.

Each quilter may determine how much piecing to do on each project. If time is not a factor, those with more experience may choose to enhance their projects with fabric blocks made up from smaller fabric blocks, pieced fabric borders, and/or pieced backs!

ADDITIONAL PROJECT DESIGNS

CONVERTING ARTWORK

Each of the projects in this publication has additional artwork featured on the page where the assembly instructions are found. This artwork has been in-cluded for use in generating new ideas. For example: when considering the project entitled "Noel Pillow," perhaps the artwork of the word "Peace" is preferred. Simply use the artwork to convert the design. Or better yet ... make both!

TEA DYEING

HOW TO MIX TEA DYE & APPLY IT TO FABRICS

Place one jar instant tea and approximately six tablespoons instant coffee into a stew kettle filled with water.

Heat over medium temperature until mixture is hot, but not boiling.

Immerse fabric in tea dye to soak for at least 30 minutes. When the fabric has been dyed to the desired color, remove it from the kettle of tea dye and wring out. When possible, hang the fabric outside to air dry — this will make the dye darker.

When applying tea dye to fabrics, do not put light-colored fabrics and dark-colored fabrics together.

All types of fabrics can be tea-dyed, but muslin is most commonly used.

If it is desired to tea-dye a project once it has been completed, place the tea dye mixture into a spray bottle, spray the project, and let it air dry.

GLOSSARY OF DECORATIVE STITCHES

BLANKET STITCH

Bring needle up at "a"; go down at "b". Bring needle up again at "c" keeping thread under needle. Go down at "d" and repeat. Make all stitches equal in size and shape.

BUTTONHOLE STITCH

Bring needle up at "a"; go down at "b". Bring needle up again at "c" keeping thread under needle. Go down at "d" and repeat. Make all stitches equal in size and shape.

This stitch is similar to the blanket stitch, but the stitches are placed closer together.

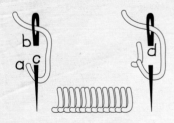

CROSS STITCH

Bring needle up at "a"; go down at "b" forming a diagonal straight stitch to any desired length. Cross the stitch with an equal-sized diagonal straight stitch coming up at "c" and going down at "d".

FRENCH KNOTS

Bring needle up at "a". Smoothly wrap floss around needle once or twice. Hold floss securely off to one side and push needle down at "b".

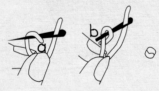

HERRINGBONE STITCH

Working from right to left, bring needle up at "a"; go down at "b". Bring needle up again at "c" making a small horizontal backstitch in back of fabric. Go down at "d" and repeat, alternating from side to side.

LAZY DAISY STITCH

Bring needle up at "a" and form a loop. Go down at "b" as close to "a" as possible, but not into "a". Come up at "c" and bring tip of needle over thread. Go down at "d" making a small anchor stitch.

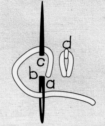

SATIN STITCH

Bring needle up at "a"; go down at "b" forming a straight stitch to any desired length. Bring needle up again at "c" and go down again at "d" forming another smooth straight stitch that slightly overlaps the first straight stitch. Repeat until design area has been filled.

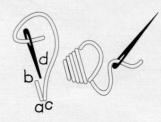

STEM STITCH

Working from left to right, bring needle up at "a"; go down at "b" forming a slightly slanting straight stitch to any desired length. Bring needle up again at "c" which is at the midpoint of the previous stitch. Go down at "d" and repeat. Make all stitches equal in size.

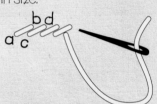

STRAIGHT STITCH

Bring needle up at "a"; go down at "b" forming a straight stitch to any desired length. Bring needle up again at "c". Go down at "d" and repeat. Make all stitches equal in size.

This stitch can also be called the running stitch and/or the back stitch. However, back stitches generally touch.

STAR QUILT

Materials:

Fusible web
Coordinating
  fabric scraps
Coordinating
  fabric blocks,
  a,b,c,d,e,f,g,h,j,k,
  m,n,p,q,r,s:
  $4\frac{1}{2}$" square (16)
Backing fabric,
  $16\frac{1}{2}$" square
Cotton batting,
  $16\frac{1}{2}$" square
Embroidery floss,
  coordinating
  color(s)
Mismatched
  buttons (7)
Pearl cotton

Assembly:

1. Before beginning, carefully read General Instructions on pages 10-22.

2. Machine-stitch $4\frac{1}{2}$" square fabric blocks together, as shown in diagram, to make quilt front.

3. Trace seven stars from page 104 onto fusible web.

4. Apply fusible web with traced patterns onto back sides of fabric scraps and cut out designs.

5. Remove backing from fusible web and adhere designs onto quilt front as shown in photograph on page 24.

6. Place embellished quilt front on top of cotton batting. Using two strands of embroidery floss, outline designs, stitching through both layers. Use decorative stitches as desired.

7. Leaving an opening for turning, finish quilt by machine-stitching backing fabric to quilt front with right sides together. Turn right side out.

8. Using two strands of embroidery floss, whip-stitch opening closed.

9. Using pearl cotton, attach buttons at center of stars, stitching through all layers.

10. Quilt through $4\frac{1}{2}$" fabric blocks without fused stars, by machine or by hand, through all layers.

a	b	c	d
e	f	g	h
j	k	m	n
p	q	r	s

Star
Quilt
Diagram

MEOWY CHRISTMAS PILLOW

Materials:

Fusible web
Coordinating fabric scraps
Tea-dyed muslin, 10" x 8"
Backing fabric, 10" x 8"
Cotton batting, 10" x 8"
Polyester stuffing
Embroidery floss, coordinating color(s)
Mismatched buttons (2)
Fade-away pen
Fine-point permanent marker

Assembly:

1. Before beginning, carefully read General Instructions on pages 10-22.

2. Trace cat, cat's tail, and star from page 104 onto fusible web.

3. Apply fusible web with traced patterns onto back sides of fabric scraps and cut out designs.

4. Remove backing from fusible web and adhere designs onto tea-dyed muslin as shown in photograph on page 26.

5. Using a fade-away pen, trace tree and phrase from page 104 onto pillow front.

6. Using a fine-point permanent marker, trace over transferred phrase.

7. Place embellished pillow front on top of cotton batting. Using two strands of embroidery floss, outline designs, stitching through both layers. Use decorative stitches as desired.

8. Using three strands of embroidery floss, stitch the tree. Add berries using French knots.

9. Using two strands of embroidery floss, attach buttons to make cat's eyes.

10. Leaving an opening for turning, finish pillow by machine-stitching backing fabric to quilted pillow front with right sides together.

11. Turn right side out and stuff pillow with polyester stuffing.

12. Using two strands of embroidery floss, whip-stitch opening closed.

13. Using six strands of embroidery floss, tie corners, stitching through all layers.

27

ANGEL BOX

Materials:

Papier-mâché box,
  7" square
Fusible web
Coordinating
  fabric scraps
Tea-dyed muslin,
  7" x 7"
Coordinating
  fabric strip,
  1" x 29"
Mismatched
  buttons (3)
Fine-point
  permanent
  marker
Craft glue
Acrylic paint, red
Cosmetic sponge

Assembly:

1. Before beginning, carefully read General Instructions on pages 10-22.

2. Trace angel's head and wings, trumpet, one large star, two medium stars, and four hearts from page 105 onto fusible web.

3. Apply fusible web with traced patterns onto back sides of fabric scraps and cut out designs. Apply fusible web onto back sides of tea-dyed muslin and fabric strip.

4. Remove backing from fusible web and adhere tea-dyed muslin onto top of papier-mâché box lid. Adhere fabric strip around all outside edges of box lid.

5. Next, adhere designs onto box lid and sides as shown in photograph on page 28.

6. Transfer the word "joy" from page 105 onto box lid.

7. Using a fine-point permanent marker, outline tea-dyed muslin and designs with hand-drawn stitches. Draw hair on angel and trace over transferred word "joy."

8. Using craft glue, adhere buttons to box lid as shown in photograph.

9. Using red acrylic paint and a cosmetic sponge, lightly add "blush" to angel's cheeks.

MITTEN PILLOW

Materials:

Fusible web
Coordinating
    fabric scraps
Coordinating
    fabric borders,
    a: $1\frac{1}{2}$" x $10\frac{1}{2}$" (1)
    b,c: $1\frac{1}{2}$" x $9\frac{1}{2}$" (2)
    d: $1\frac{1}{2}$" x $8\frac{1}{2}$" (1)
Coordinating
    fabric blocks,
    e,f,g,h:
    $4\frac{1}{2}$" square (4)
Backing fabric,
    $10\frac{1}{2}$" square
Cotton batting,
    $10\frac{1}{2}$" square
Polyester stuffing
Embroidery floss,
    coordinating
    color(s)
Button

Assembly:

1. Before beginning, carefully read General Instructions on pages 10-22.

2. Machine-stitch fabric borders and fabric blocks together, as shown in diagram, to make pillow front.

3. Trace mitten, mitten's cuff, and heart from page 107 onto fusible web.

4. Apply fusible web with traced patterns onto back sides of fabric scraps and cut out designs.

5. Remove backing from fusible web and adhere designs onto pillow front as shown in photograph on page 30.

6. Place embellished pillow front on top of cotton batting. Using two strands of embroidery floss, outline designs, stitching through both layers. Use decorative stitches as desired.

7. Using three strands of embroidery floss, stitch a large "X" on one side of heart.

8. Using two strands of embroidery floss, attach button in center of heart.

9. Leaving an opening for turning, finish pillow by machine-stitching backing fabric to quilted pillow front with right sides together.

10. Turn right side out and stuff pillow with polyester stuffing.

11. Using two strands of embroidery floss, whip-stitch opening closed.

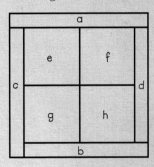

Mitten
Pillow
Diagram

GINGERBREAD MAN ORNAMENT

Materials:

Fusible web
Coordinating fabric scraps
Coordinating fabric block, 8" x 5"
Backing fabric, 8" x 5"
Cotton batting, 8" x 5"
Embroidery floss, coordinating color(s)
Mismatched buttons (3)
Pearl cotton
Fabric stiffener

Assembly:

1. Before beginning, carefully read General Instructions on pages 10-22.

2. Trace gingerbread man and heart from page 108 onto fusible web.

3. Apply fusible web with traced patterns onto back sides of fabric scraps and cut out designs.

4. Remove backing from fusible web and adhere designs onto 8" x 5" fabric block as shown in photograph on page 32.

5. Place embellished ornament front on top of cotton batting. Using three strands of embroidery floss, outline designs, stitching through both layers. Use decorative stitches as desired.

6. Using three strands of embroidery floss, stitch a large "X" on one side of heart.

7. Using two strands of embroidery floss, attach two buttons to make gingerbread man's eyes. Attach one button in center of heart.

8. Leaving an opening for turning, finish ornament by machine-stitching backing fabric to quilted ornament front with right sides together. Turn right side out.

9. Using two strands of embroidery floss, whip-stitch opening closed.

10. Using pearl cotton, stitch through top of ornament and knot in front to make a loop for hanging.

11. Using fabric stiffener, stiffen ornament following manufacturer's directions.

NOEL PILLOW

Materials:

Fusible web
Coordinating fabric scraps
Coordinating fabric blocks, a,b,c,d,e: $6\frac{1}{2}" \times 3\frac{1}{2}"$ (5)
Backing fabric, $6\frac{1}{2}" \times 15\frac{1}{2}"$
Cotton batting, $6\frac{1}{2}" \times 15\frac{1}{2}"$
Polyester stuffing
Embroidery floss, coordinating color(s)

Assembly:

1. Before beginning, carefully read General Instructions on pages 10-22.

2. Machine-stitch fabric blocks together, as shown in diagram, to make pillow front.

3. Trace letters "n-o-e-l" and heart from page 109 onto fusible web.

4. Apply fusible web with traced letters and heart onto back sides of fabric scraps and cut out designs.

5. Remove backing from fusible web and adhere designs onto pillow front as shown in photograph on page 34.

6. Place embellished pillow front on top of cotton batting. Using two strands of embroidery floss, outline designs, stitching through both layers. Use decorative stitches as desired.

7. Leaving an opening for turning, finish pillow by machine-stitching backing fabric to quilted pillow front with right sides together.

8. Turn right side out and stuff pillow with polyester stuffing.

9. Using two strands of embroidery floss, whip-stitch opening closed.

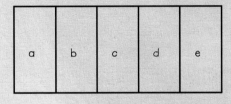

a	b	c	d	e

Noel Pillow Diagram

STAR PILLOW

Materials:

Fusible web
Coordinating
   fabric scraps
Coordinating
   fabric blocks,
   a,b,c,d:
   5" square (4)
Backing fabric,
   9½" square
Cotton batting,
   9½" square
Polyester stuffing
Embroidery floss,
   coordinating
   color(s)
Button
Pearl cotton

Assembly:

1. Before beginning, carefully read General Instructions on pages 10-22.

2. Machine-stitch fabric blocks together, as shown in diagram, to make pillow front.

3. Trace pieces of star from page 110 onto fusible web.

4. Apply fusible web with traced patterns onto back sides of fabric scraps and cut out designs.

5. Remove backing from fusible web and adhere designs onto pillow front as shown in photograph on page 36.

6. Place embellished pillow front on top of cotton batting. Using two strands of embroidery floss, outline designs, stitching through both layers. Use decorative stitches as desired.

7. Leaving an opening for turning, finish pillow by machine-stitching backing fabric to quilted pillow front with right sides together.

8. Turn right side out and stuff pillow with polyester stuffing.

9. Using two strands of embroidery floss, whip-stitch opening closed.

10. Using pearl cotton, attach button at center of star, stitching through all layers.

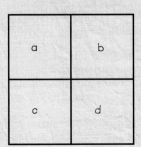

Star
Pillow
Diagram

christmas is what you make of it.

PRIMITIVE CHRISTMAS TREE ORNAMENT

Materials:

Coordinating
  fabric borders,
  a: 1" x 3½" (1)
  b: 1" x 4" (1)
  c: 1" x 8" (1)
  d: 1" x 7½" (1)
Coordinating
  fabric blocks,
  e: 2⅜" square (3)
  f: 2⅜" square (3)
  g: 2" x 1¾" (2)
  h: 2" x 1" (1)
Backing fabric,
  7½" x 4½"
Cotton batting,
  7½" x 4½"
Embroidery floss,
  coordinating
  color(s)
Pearl cotton
Fabric stiffener

Assembly:

1. Before beginning, carefully read General Instructions on pages 10-22.

2. Cut all six 2⅜" square fabric blocks in half, diagonally, to make twelve fabric triangles.

3. Machine-stitch fabric triangles, both 2" x 1¾" fabric blocks, and the 2" x 1" fabric block together, as shown in diagram, to make center fabric block.

4. Machine-stitch fabric borders and center fabric block together to make ornament front.

5. Place pieced ornament front on top of cotton batting. Using three strands of embroidery floss, outline center fabric block and design, stitching through both layers. Use decorative stitches as desired.

6. Leaving an opening for turning, finish ornament by machine-stitching backing fabric to quilted ornament front with right sides together. Turn right side out.

7. Using two strands of embroidery floss, whip-stitch opening closed.

8. Using pearl cotton, stitch through top of ornament and knot in front to make a loop for hanging.

9. Using fabric stiffener, stiffen ornament following manufacturer's directions.

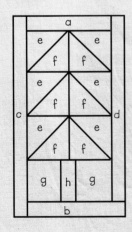

Primitive
Christmas
Tree
Ornament
Diagram

SNOWMAN STOCKING ORNAMENT

Materials:

Fusible web
Coordinating
    fabric scraps
Coordinating
    fabric blocks,
    $1^1/_2$" square (18)
    $2^1/_2$" x $4^1/_2$" (2)
    9" x 13" (2)
Embroidery floss,
    coordinating
    color(s)
Mismatched
    buttons (3)
Pearl cotton
Fade-away pen

Assembly:

1. Before beginning, carefully read General Instructions on pages 10-22.

2. Using a fade-away pen, trace stocking from page 111 onto 9" x 13" fabric blocks and cut out.

3. Machine-stitch one $2^1/_2$" x $4^1/_2$" fabric block to top edge of stocking front. Repeat for stocking back.

4. Machine-stitch $1^1/_2$" square fabric blocks together to make one pieced $6^1/_2$" x $3^1/_2$" fabric block (six down; three across).

5. Trace snowman, snowman's arms and scarf, stocking toe, and stocking heel from page 111 onto fusible web.

6. Apply fusible web with traced snowman onto back side of pieced fabric block and cut out. Apply fusible web with remaining traced patterns onto back sides of fabric scraps and cut out designs.

7. Remove backing from fusible web and adhere designs onto stocking front as shown in photograph on page 40.

8. Using two strands of embroidery floss, outline designs. Use decorative stitches as desired.

9. Using two strands of embroidery floss, attach buttons to snowman.

10. Fold top edges of stocking front and stocking back to wrong side's seam line. Leaving an opening at the top, finish stocking by machine-stitching stocking front to stocking back with right sides together. Turn right side out.

11. Using pearl cotton, stitch through top back corner of stocking and knot to make a loop for hanging.

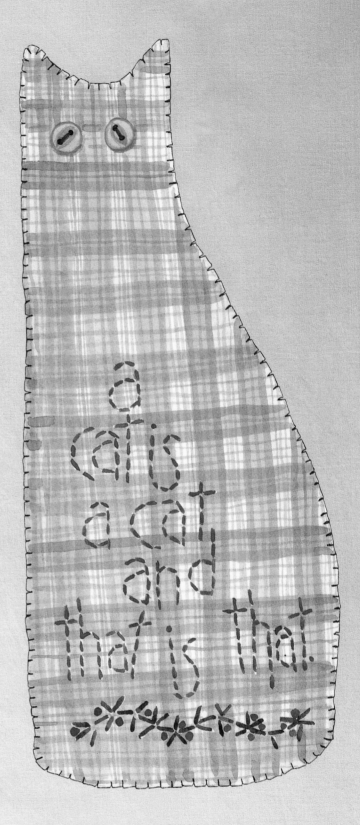

angels remind you
that you are enough.

ANGEL KITTY PILLOW

Materials:

Tea-dyed muslin,
 6" x 7"
Backing fabric,
 6" x 7"
Cotton batting,
 6" x 7"
Polyester stuffing
Embroidery floss,
 coordinating
 color(s)
Pearl cotton
Fade-away pen

Assembly:

1. Before beginning, carefully read General Instructions on pages 10-22.

2. Using a fade-away pen, trace kitty and kitty's star halo from page 110 onto tea-dyed muslin.

3. Place tea-dyed muslin on top of cotton batting. Using three strands of embroidery floss, stitch designs, stitching through both layers. Use decorative stitches as desired.

4. Using two strands of embroidery floss, stitch eyes on kitty and berries on wreath using French knots. Stitch nose on kitty using satin stitches.

5. Leaving an opening for turning, finish pillow by machine-stitching backing fabric to quilted pillow front with right sides together.

6. Turn right side out and stuff pillow with polyester stuffing.

7. Using two strands of embroidery floss, whip-stitch opening closed.

8. Using pearl cotton, tie corners, stitching through all layers.

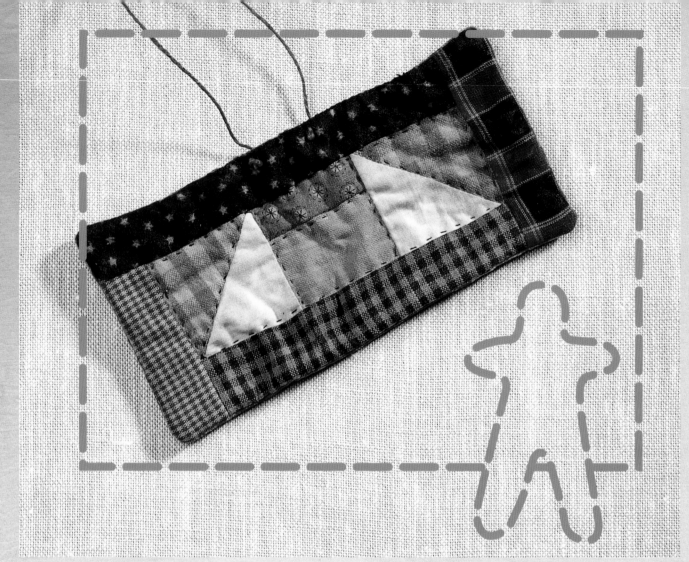

You give but little of Yourself
when You give of Your possessions.
it is when You give of Your heart
and from Your hands
that You truly give.

PRIMITIVE ANGEL ORNAMENT

Materials:

Coordinating
  fabric borders,
  a: 1" x 6" (1)
  b: 1" x 5$\frac{1}{2}$" (1)
  c: 1" x 3" (1)
  d: 1" x 3$\frac{1}{2}$" (1)
Coordinating
  fabric blocks,
  e: 2$\frac{3}{8}$" square (1)
  f: 2$\frac{3}{8}$" square (1)
  g: 1" x 2" (1)
  h: 1$\frac{1}{2}$" x 2" (1)
Backing fabric,
  3$\frac{1}{2}$" x 6$\frac{1}{2}$"
Cotton batting,
  3$\frac{1}{2}$" x 6$\frac{1}{2}$"
Embroidery floss,
  coordinating
  color(s)
Pearl cotton
Fabric stiffener

Assembly:

1. Before beginning, carefully read General Instructions on pages 10-22.

2. Cut both 2$\frac{3}{8}$" square fabric blocks in half, diagonally, to make four fabric triangles.

3. Machine-stitch fabric triangles, 1" x 2" fabric block, and 1$\frac{1}{2}$" x 2" fabric block together, as shown in diagram, to make center fabric block.

4. Machine-stitch fabric borders and center fabric block together to make ornament front.

5. Place pieced ornament front on top of cotton batting. Using three strands of embroidery floss, outline center fabric block, 2" x 2$\frac{1}{2}$" fabric block, and along each diagonal, stitching through both layers. Use decorative stitches as desired.

6. Leaving an opening for turning, finish ornament by machine-stitching backing fabric to quilted ornament front with right sides together. Turn right side out.

7. Using two strands of embroidery floss, whip-stitch opening closed.

8. Using pearl cotton, stitch through top of ornament and knot in front to make a loop for hanging.

9. Using fabric stiffener, stiffen ornament following manufacturer's directions.

Primitive
Angel
Ornament
Diagram

REJOICE QUILT

Materials:

Fusible web
Coordinating
  fabric scraps
Coordinating
  fabric borders,
  a,b: 2" x 9½" (2)
  c,d: 2" x 21½" (2)
Coordinating
  fabric blocks,
  e,f,g,h,j,k,m:
  6½" x 3½" (7)
  n: 6½" square (1)
Backing fabric,
  21½" x 12½"
Cotton batting,
  21½" x 12½"
Embroidery floss,
  coordinating
  color(s)

Assembly:

1. Before beginning, carefully read General Instructions on pages 10-22.

2. Machine-stitch fabric borders and fabric blocks together, as shown in diagram, to make quilt front.

3. Trace letters "r-e-j-o-i-c-e" and angel's head, cheeks and wings, trumpet, one large star, and three small stars from pages 105-106 onto fusible web.

4. Apply fusible web with traced letters and patterns onto back sides of fabric scraps and cut out designs.

5. Remove backing from fusible web and adhere designs onto quilt front as shown in photograph on page 46.

6. Place embellished quilt front on top of cotton batting.

Using two strands of embroidery floss, outline designs, stitching through both layers. Use decorative stitches as desired.

7. Leaving an opening for turning, finish quilt by machine-stitching backing fabric to quilt front with right sides together. Turn right side out.

8. Using two strands of embroidery floss, whip-stitch opening closed.

9. Quilt around fabric blocks, by machine or by hand, through all layers.

Rejoice
Quilt
Diagram

SEASON'S GREETINGS PILLOW

Materials:

Fusible web
Coordinating fabric scraps
Coordinating fabric borders,
  a,b: 2" x 18½" (2)
  c,d: 2" x 10" (2)
Coordinating fabric block,
  e: 7" x 18½" (1)
Backing fabric,
  10" x 21½"
Cotton batting,
  10" x 21½"
Polyester stuffing
Embroidery floss,
  coordinating color(s)
Mismatched buttons (4)
Pearl cotton
Fade-away pen

Assembly:

1. Before beginning, carefully read General Instructions on pages 10-22.

2. Machine-stitch fabric borders and fabric block together, as shown in diagram, to make pillow front.

3. Trace letters "s and g" from page 112 onto fusible web.

4. Apply fusible web with traced letters onto back sides of fabric scraps and cut out designs.

5. Remove backing from fusible web and adhere designs onto pillow front as shown in photograph on page 48.

6. Using a fade-away pen, trace remaining letters "e-a-s-o-n-'-s r-e-e-t-i-n-g-s" from page 112 onto pillow front.

7. Place embellished pillow front on top of cotton batting. Using two strands of embroidery floss, outline center fabric block and designs, stitching through both layers. Use decorative stitches as desired.

8. Using three strands of embroidery floss, stitch the letters "eason's reetings."

9. Leaving an opening for turning, finish pillow by machine-stitching backing fabric to quilted pillow front with right sides together.

10. Turn right side out and stuff pillow with polyester stuffing.

11. Using two strands of embroidery floss, whip-stitch opening closed.

12. Using pearl cotton, attach buttons at corners where fabric borders connect, stitching through all layers.

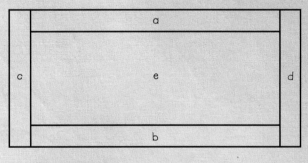

Season's Greetings Pillow Diagram

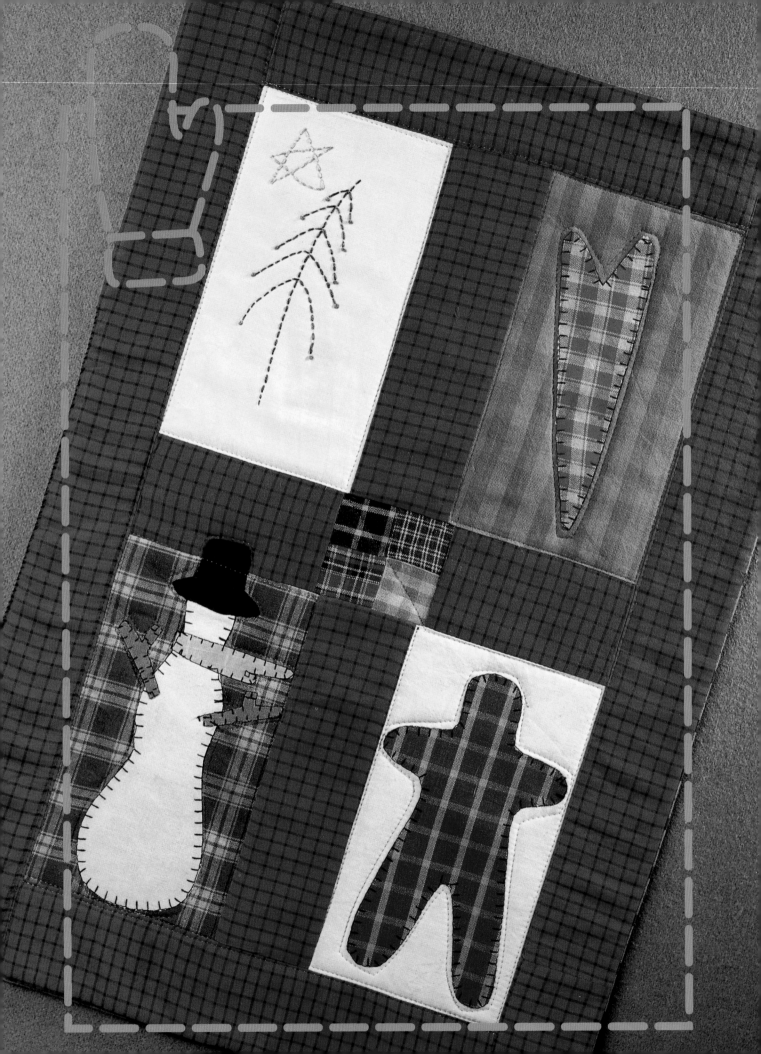

FOUR-PATCH CHRISTMAS QUILT

Materials:

Fusible web
Coordinating
   fabric scraps
Matching
   fabric borders,
   a,b: $2^1/2$" x $10^1/2$" (2)
   c,d: $2^1/2$" x $20^1/2$" (2)
Coordinating
   fabric blocks,
   e,f: 3" x $4^1/4$" (2)
   g,h: 3" x $7^1/4$" (2)
   j,k,m,n:
   $7^1/2$" x $4^1/2$" (4)
   p,q,r,s:
   $1^1/2$" square (4)
Backing fabric,
   $20^1/2$" x $14^1/2$"
Cotton batting,
   $20^1/2$" x $14^1/2$"
Embroidery floss,
   coordinating
   color(s)
Fade-away pen

Assembly:

1.   Before beginning, carefully read General Instructions on pages 10-22.

2.   Machine-stitch fabric borders and fabric blocks together, as shown in diagram, to make quilt front.

3.   Trace heart, snowman, snowman's arms, scarf, and hat from page 121 and gingerbread man from page 108 onto fusible web.

4.   Apply fusible web with traced patterns onto back sides of fabric scraps and cut out designs.

5.   Remove backing from fusible web and adhere designs onto quilt front as shown in photograph on page 50.

6.   Using a fade-away pen, trace tree and star from page 121 onto quilt front.

7.   Place embellished quilt front on top of cotton batting. Using two strands of embroidery floss, outline designs, stitching through both layers. Use decorative stitches as desired.

8.   Using three strands of embroidery floss, stitch the tree and star. Add berries using French knots.

9.   Leaving an opening for turning, finish quilt by machine-stitching backing fabric to quilt front with right sides together. Turn right side out.

10.   Using two strands of embroidery floss, whip-stitch opening closed.

11.   Quilt around fabric blocks and designs by machine, or by hand, through all layers.

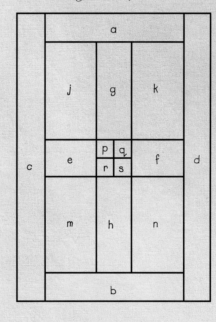

Four-Patch
Christmas
Quilt
Diagram

KEEP YOUR HEART MERRY PILLOW

Materials:

Fusible web
Coordinating
   fabric scraps
Coordinating
   fabric block,
   10" x 9"
Backing fabric,
   10" x 9"
Cotton batting,
   10" x 9"
Polyester stuffing
Embroidery floss,
   coordinating
   color(s)
Button
Fade-away pen

Assembly:

1. Before beginning, carefully read General Instructions on pages 10-22.

2. Trace large heart, small heart, and star from page 113 onto fusible web.

3. Apply fusible web with traced patterns onto back sides of fabric scraps and cut out designs.

4. Remove backing from fusible web and adhere designs onto 10" x 9" fabric block as shown in photograph on page 52.

5. Using a fade-away pen, trace vine and words "keep your merry" from page 113 onto pillow front.

6. Place embellished pillow front on top of cotton batting. Using two strands of embroidery floss, outline designs, stitching through both layers. Use decorative stitches as desired.

7. Using three strands of embroidery floss, stitch the vine.

Add berries using French knots.

8. Using three strands of embroidery floss, stitch the words "keep your merry."

9. Using two strands of embroidery floss, attach button in upper right hand corner of small heart.

10. Leaving an opening for turning, finish pillow by machine-stitching backing fabric to quilted pillow front with right sides together.

11. Turn right side out and stuff pillow with polyester stuffing.

12. Using two strands of embroidery floss, whip-stitch opening closed.

13. Using six strands of embroidery floss, tie corners, stitching through all layers.

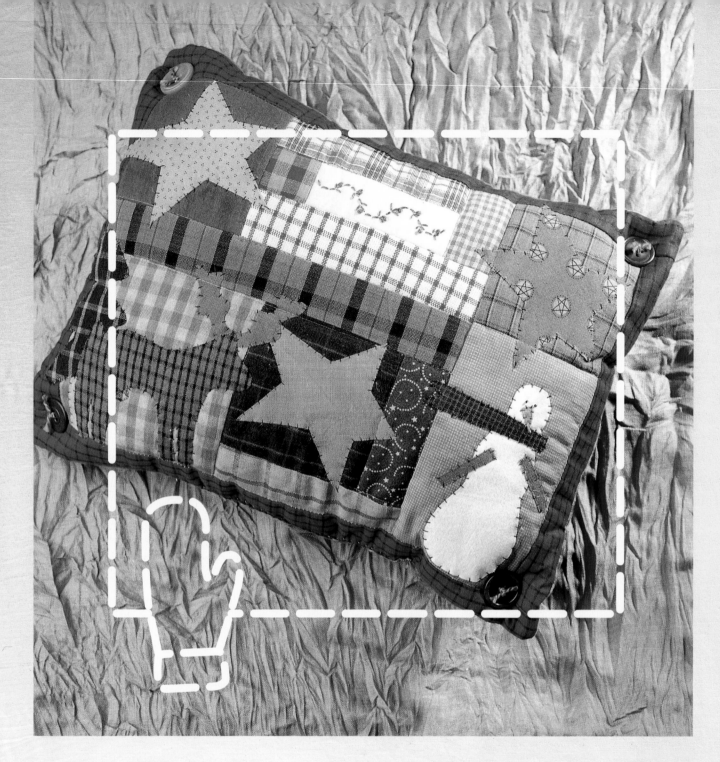

wish upon
a christmas star.

CHRISTMAS PILLOW

Materials:

Fusible web
Coordinating
   fabric scraps
Coordinating
   fabric borders,
   a,b: $1\frac{1}{2}$" x $13\frac{1}{2}$" (2)
   c,d: $1\frac{1}{2}$" x $10\frac{1}{2}$" (2)
Coordinating
   fabric blocks,
   e: $1\frac{1}{2}$" square (1)
   f: $1\frac{1}{2}$" x $2\frac{1}{2}$" (1)
   g,h: $1\frac{1}{2}$" x $3\frac{1}{2}$" (2)
   j,k: $1\frac{1}{2}$" x $4\frac{1}{2}$" (2)
   m: $1\frac{1}{2}$" x $5\frac{1}{2}$" (1)
   n: $1\frac{1}{2}$" x $8\frac{1}{2}$" (1)
   p,q,r: $3\frac{1}{2}$" square (3)
   s: $4\frac{1}{2}$" square (1)
   t: $5\frac{1}{2}$" x $3\frac{1}{2}$" (1)
Backing fabric,
   $10\frac{1}{2}$" x $13\frac{1}{2}$"
Cotton batting,
   $10\frac{1}{2}$" x $13\frac{1}{2}$"
Polyester stuffing
Embroidery floss,
   coordinating
   color(s)
Mismatched
   buttons (4)
Pearl cotton
Fade-away pen

Assembly:

1. Before beginning, carefully read General Instructions on pages 10-22.

2. Machine-stitch fabric borders and fabric blocks together, as shown in diagram, to make pillow front.

3. Trace tree, tree's trunk, moose, moose's antlers, snowman (without hat), snow-man's nose, scarf, and arms, and three stars from page 114 onto fusible web.

4. Apply fusible web with traced patterns onto back sides of fabric scraps and cut out designs.

5. Remove backing from fusible web and adhere designs onto pillow front as shown in photograph on page 54.

6. Using a fade-away pen, trace vine from page 114 onto pillow front.

7. Place embellished pillow front on top of cotton batting. Using two strands of embroidery floss, outline designs, stitching through both layers. Use decorative stitches as desired.

8. Using three strands of embroidery floss, stitch the vine. Add berries using French knots.

9. Using two strands of embroidery floss, stitch eyes on snowman using French knots.

10. Leaving an opening for turning, finish pillow by machine-stitching backing fabric to quilted pillow front with right sides together.

11. Turn right side out and stuff pillow with polyester stuffing.

12. Using two strands of embroidery floss, whip-stitch opening closed.

13. Using pearl cotton, attach buttons at corners where fabric borders connect, stitching through all layers.

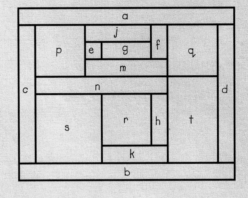

Christmas Pillow Diagram

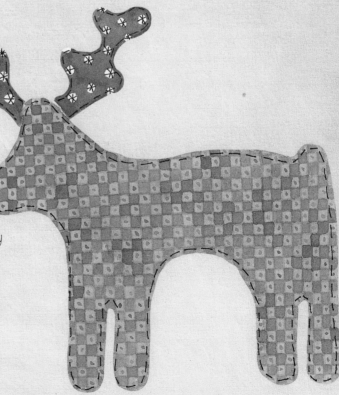

for somehow, not only at christmas,
but all the long year through,
the joy that you give to others
is the joy that comes back to you.

PRIMITIVE SANTA ORNAMENT

Materials:

Coordinating fabric borders,
 a,b: 1" x 4" (2)
 c,d: 1" x 5¼" (2)

Coordinating fabric blocks,
 e,f: 3" square (2)
 g: 1" x 2½" (1)
 h: 1¼" x 1" (2)
 j: 1¼" x 1½" (1)
 k: 2½" square (1)

Backing fabric,
 6¼" x 3½"

Cotton batting,
 6¼" x 3½"

Embroidery floss, coordinating color(s)

Pearl cotton

Fabric stiffener

Assembly:

1. Before beginning, carefully read General Instructions on pages 10-22.

2. Trace all three triangles from page 125 onto 3" square fabric blocks and cut out.

3. Machine-stitch fabric triangles, 1" x 2½" fabric block, both 1¼" x 1" fabric blocks, 1¼" x 1½" fabric block, and the 2½" x 2½" fabric block together, as shown in diagram, to make center fabric block.

4. Machine-stitch fabric borders and center fabric block together to make ornament front.

5. Place pieced ornament front on top of cotton batting. Using three strands of embroidery floss, outline center fabric block, Santa's hat and face, stitching through both layers. Use decorative stitches as desired.

6. Leaving an opening for turning, finish ornament by machine-stitching backing fabric to quilted ornament front with right sides together. Turn right side out.

7. Using two strands of embroidery floss, whip-stitch opening closed.

8. Using pearl cotton, stitch through top of ornament and knot in front to make a loop for hanging.

9. Using fabric stiffener, stiffen ornament following manufacturer's directions.

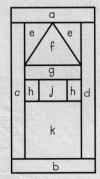

Primitive Santa Ornament Diagram

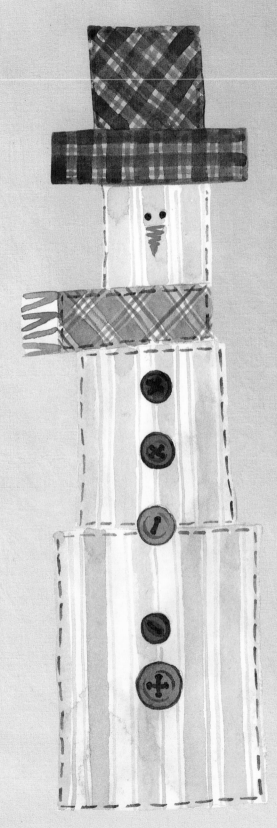

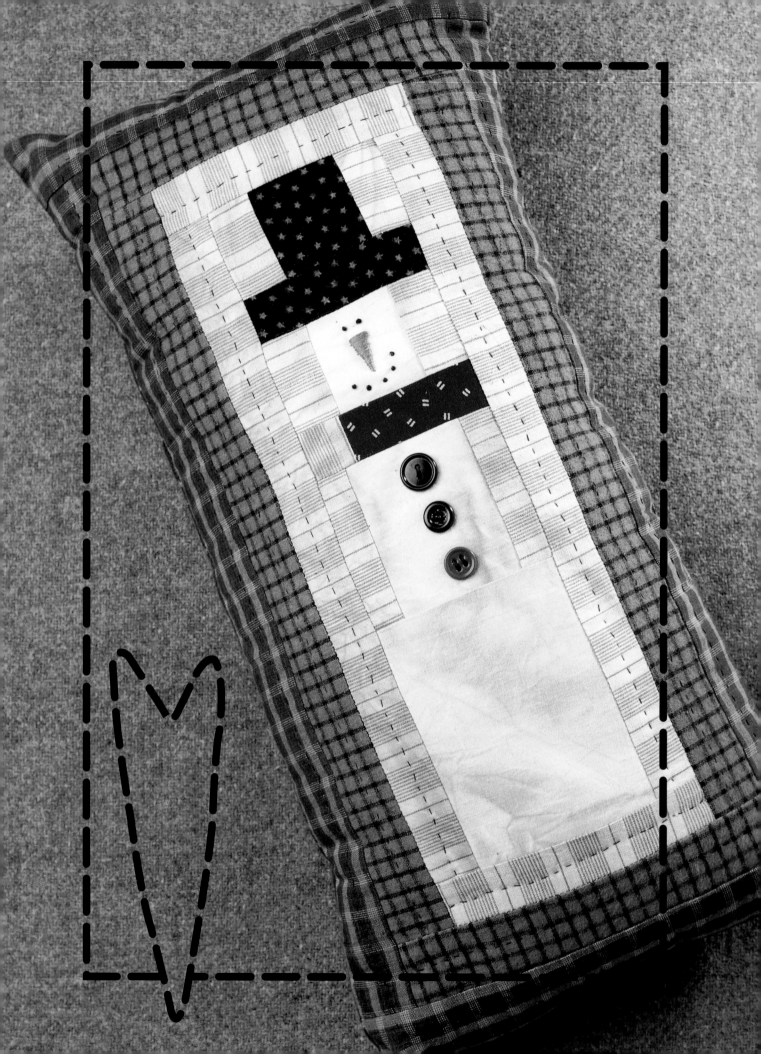

PRIMITIVE SNOWMAN PILLOW

Materials:

Coordinating
  fabric borders,
  outer:
  a,b: 2" x 10" (2)
  c,d: 2" x 15" (2)
  center:
  e,f: $1^1/2$" x 7" (2)
  g,h: $1^1/2$" x 14" (2)
  inner:
  j,k: $1^1/4$" x 5" (2)
  m,n: $1^1/4$" x $11^3/4$" (2)

Coordinating
  fabric blocks,
  p: 2" x $1^1/4$" (4)
  q: 2" square (1)
  r: $1^1/4$" x $3^1/2$" (1)
  s: 2" square (1)
  t: $1^1/4$" square (1)
  u: $1^1/4$" x $2^3/4$" (1)
  v: 3" x 1" (2)
  w: 3" x $2^1/2$" (1)
  x: $4^1/2$" x $3^1/2$" (1)

Backing fabric,
  18" x 10"
Cotton batting,
  18" x 10"
Polyester stuffing
Embroidery floss,
  coordinating
  color(s)
Mismatched
  buttons (3)

Assembly:

1. Before beginning, carefully read General Instructions on pages 10-22.

2. Machine-stitch fabric blocks together, as shown in diagram, to make center fabric block.

3. Machine-stitch all three fabric borders and center fabric block together to make pillow front.

4. Place embellished pillow front on top of cotton batting. Using two strands of embroidery floss, stitch along centers of fabric borders, stitching through both layers. Use decorative stitches as desired.

5. Using two strands of embroidery floss, stitch eyes and mouth on snowman using French knots. Stitch nose on snowman using satin stitches.

6. Using pearl cotton, attach buttons to snowman.

7. Leaving an opening for turning, finish pillow by machine-stitching backing fabric to quilted pillow front with right sides together.

8. Turn right side out and stuff pillow with polyester stuffing.

9. Using two strands of embroidery floss, whip-stitch opening closed.

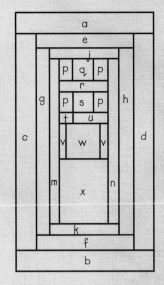

Primitive
Snowman
Pillow
Diagram

FRAMED RAGGEDY ANGEL

Materials:

Fusible web
Coordinating
    fabric scraps
Coordinating
    fabric block,
    10" x 8"
Cotton batting,
    10" x 8"
Embroidery floss,
    coordinating
    color(s)
Wooden frame,
    8" x 10"

Assembly:

1.   Before beginning, carefully read General Instructions on pages 10-22.

2.   Trace raggedy angel's face, nose, halo, wings, hands, legs, dress, apron and collar, and star patterns from page 115 onto fusible web.

3.   Apply fusible web with traced patterns onto back sides of fabric scraps and cut out designs.

4.   Remove backing from fusible web and adhere designs onto 10" x 8" fabric block as shown in photograph on page 60.

5.   Place embellished fabric block on top of cotton batting. Using two strands of embroidery floss, outline designs, stitching through both layers. Use decorative stitches as desired.

6.   Using three strands of embroidery floss, stitch eyes on angel using French knots. Stitch mouth and hair on angel using straight stitches.

7.   Place design in a wooden frame.

joy is when
love is shared.

CHRISTMAS BOX

Materials:

Papier-mâché box,
  8½" square
Fusible web
Coordinating
  fabric scraps
Coordinating
  fabric blocks,
  a: 5" square (1)
  b,c: 3½" square (2)
  d: 3½" x 1½" (1)
  e: 5" x 3½" (1)
Coordinating
  fabric strip,
  1" x 35"
Mismatched
  buttons (4)
Fine-point
  permanent
  marker
Craft glue

Assembly:

1. Before beginning, carefully read General Instructions on pages 10-22.

2. Trace tree, tree's trunk, moose, moose's antlers, cat, cat's scarf, snowman, snowman's hat, nose, scarf, and arms, and nine stars from page 114 onto fusible web.

3. Apply fusible web with traced patterns onto back sides of fabric scraps and cut out designs. Apply fusible web onto back sides of fabric blocks and fabric strip.

4. Remove backing from fusible web and adhere fabric blocks onto top of papier-mâché box lid as shown in diagram. Adhere fabric strip around all outside edges of box lid.

5. Next, adhere designs onto box lid and sides as shown in photograph on page 62.

6. Using a fine-point permanent marker, outline fabric blocks and designs with hand-drawn stitches. Draw eyes and mouth on snowman.

7. Using craft glue, adhere buttons to box lid as shown in photograph.

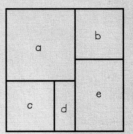

Christmas
Box
Diagram

63

angels believe in you.

FLYING ANGEL PILLOW

Materials:

Fusible web
Coordinating
    fabric scraps
Tea-dyed muslin,
    8" x 13"
Backing fabric,
    8" x 13"
Cotton batting,
    8" x 13"
Polyester stuffing
Embroidery floss,
    coordinating
    color(s)
Fade-away pen

Assembly:

1.   Before beginning, carefully read General Instructions on pages 10-22.

2.   Trace angel's face, wings (one in reverse), hand, legs, dress and sleeve, and star from page 116 onto fusible web.

3.   Apply fusible web with traced patterns onto back sides of fabric scraps and cut out designs.

4.   Remove backing from fusible web and adhere designs onto tea-dyed muslin as shown in photograph on page 64.

5.   Using a fade-away pen, trace angel's halo and wreath from page 116 onto pillow front.

6.   Place embellished pillow front on top of cotton batting. Using two strands of embroidery floss, outline designs, stitching through both layers. Use decorative stitches as desired.

7.   Using three strands of embroidery floss, stitch the halo and the wreath. Add berries using French Knots.

8.   Leaving an opening for turning, finish pillow by machine-stitching backing fabric to quilted pillow front with right sides together.

9.   Turn right side out and stuff pillow with polyester stuffing.

10.   Using two strands of embroidery floss, whip-stitch opening closed.

11.   Using six strands of embroidery floss, tie corners, stitching through all layers.

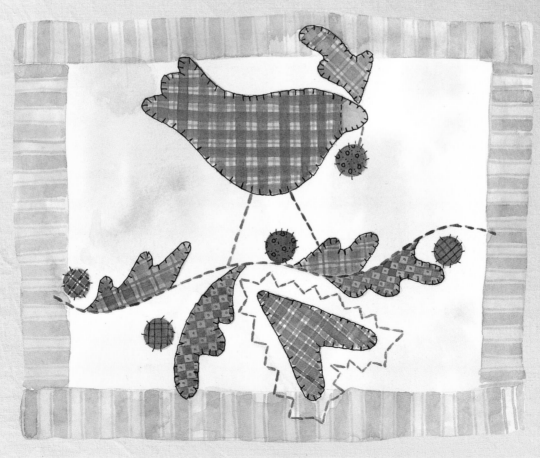

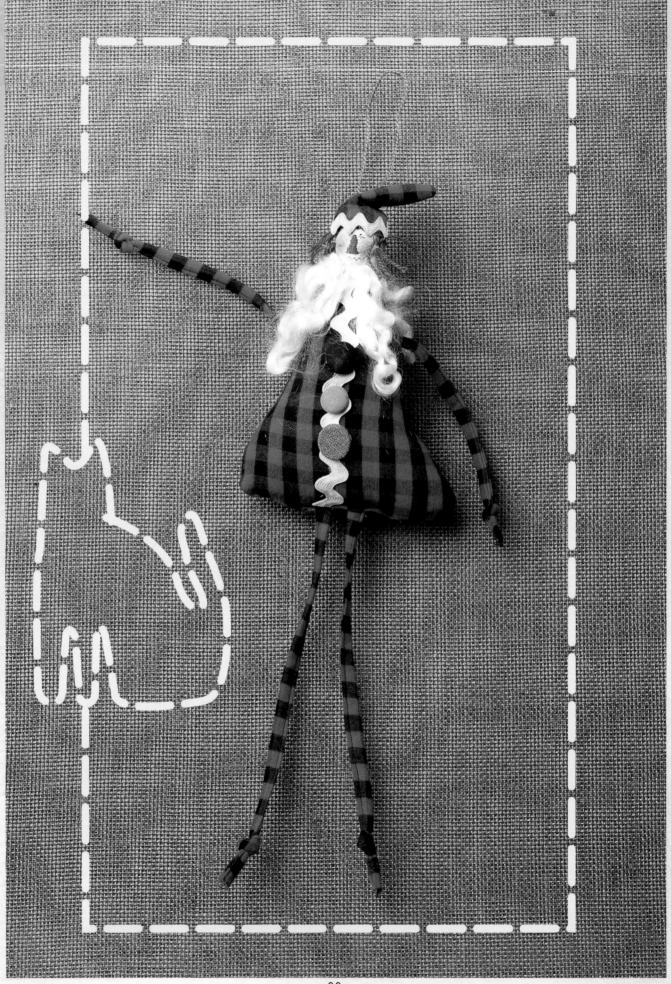

RAGGEDY SANTA ORNAMENT

Materials:

Tea-dyed muslin,
    $2\frac{1}{2}$" x $6\frac{1}{2}$" (2)
Coordinating
    fabric blocks,
    $2\frac{1}{2}$" x 3" (2)
    $6\frac{1}{2}$" square (2)
Coordinating
    fabric strip,
    $1\frac{1}{4}$" x 45"
Polyester stuffing
Beard fur
Ric-rac
Embroidery floss,
    coordinating
    color(s)
Mismatched
    buttons (3)
Pearl cotton
Fine-point
    permanent
    marker
Craft glue

Assembly:

1.   Before beginning, carefully read General Instructions on pages 10-22.

2.   Machine-stitch one piece tea-dyed muslin to one $6\frac{1}{2}$" square fabric block to make Santa's front. Repeat for Santa's back.

3.   Fold both long edges of fabric strip in $\frac{1}{4}$". Fold strip in half, lengthwise, and machine-stitch. Cut fabric strip into four lengths to make Santa's arms and legs.

4.   With right sides of pieced fabric blocks together, trace Santa from page 118 onto one fabric block.

5.   Place arms and legs in position (on the inside) as indicated.

Leaving an opening for turning, finish Santa by machine-stitching along traced lines.

6.   Trim seam allowance back to $\frac{1}{8}$" and clip corners. Turn right side out and stuff Santa with polyester stuffing.

7.   Using two strands of embroidery floss, whip-stitch opening closed.

8.   Knot arms and legs at desired lengths and cut off excess.

9.   With right sides of $2\frac{1}{2}$" x 3" fabric blocks together, trace Santa's hat from page 118 onto one fabric block.

10.   Leaving bottom edge open, finish Santa's hat by machine-stitching along traced lines.

11.   Trim seam allowance back to $\frac{1}{8}$". Turn right side out.

12.   Using two strands of embroidery floss, stitch nose on Santa using satin stitches.

13.   Using pearl cotton, stitch hair on Santa and cut to desired length.

14.   Using a fine-point permanent marker, draw eyes and mouth on Santa.

15.   Using craft glue, adhere ric-rac down front of Santa and around edge of Santa's hat. Glue Santa's hat in place. Add Santa's beard. Glue buttons on top of ric-rac down front of Santa.

16.   Using pearl cotton, stitch through back of Santa's head and knot to make a loop for hanging.

just bee cause
it's christmas and i love you.

MERRY BEE PILLOW

Materials:

Fusible web
Coordinating
    fabric scraps
Coordinating
    fabric borders,
    a,b: $1^1/_2$" x $12^1/_2$" (2)
    c,d: $1^1/_2$" x $7^1/_2$" (2)
Coordinating
    fabric blocks,
    e: $1^1/_2$" x $6^1/_2$" (1)
    f,g: $6^1/_2$" x $3^1/_2$" (2)
    h: $7^1/_2$" x $4^1/_2$" (1)
Backing fabric,
    $9^1/_2$" x $12^1/_2$"
Cotton batting,
    $9^1/_2$" x $12^1/_2$"
Polyester stuffing
Embroidery floss,
    coordinating
    color(s)
Mismatched
    buttons (4)
Pearl cotton
Fade-away pen

Assembly:

1. Before beginning, carefully read General Instructions on pages 10-22.

2. Machine-stitch fabric borders and fabric blocks together, as shown in diagram, to make pillow front.

3. Trace beehive, beehive's opening, gingerbread man, and heart from page 108 onto fusible web.

4. Apply fusible web with traced patterns onto back sides of fabric scraps and cut out designs.

5. Remove backing from fusible web and adhere designs onto pillow front as shown in photograph on page 68.

6. Using a fade-away pen, trace words "merry bee" from page 108 onto pillow front.

7. Place embellished pillow front on top of cotton batting. Using two strands of embroidery floss, outline fabric blocks and designs, stitching through both layers. Use decorative stitches as desired.

8. Using three strands of embroidery floss, stitch the words "merry bee."

9. Using two strands of embroidery floss, stitch the bee's wings using lazy-daisy stitches and bee's body using a French knot. Stitch eyes on gingerbread man using French knots.

10. Leaving an opening for turning, finish pillow by machine-stitching backing fabric to quilted pillow front with right sides together.

11. Turn right side out and stuff pillow with polyester stuffing.

12. Using two strands of embroidery floss, whip-stitch opening closed.

13. Using pearl cotton, attach buttons at corners where fabric borders connect, stitching through all layers.

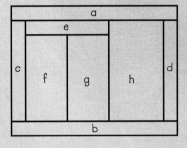

Merry
Bee
Pillow
Diagram

HEART STOCKING ORNAMENT

Materials:

Fusible web
Coordinating
    fabric scraps
Coordinating
    fabric blocks,
    $2^1/2$" x $1^1/2$" (6)
    7" x 11" (2)
Embroidery floss,
    coordinating
    color(s)
Pearl cotton
Fade-away pen

Assembly:

1. Before beginning, carefully read General Instructions on pages 10-22.

2. Using a fade-away pen, trace stocking from page 120 onto 7" x 11" fabric blocks and cut out.

3. Machine-stitch three $2^1/2$" x $1^1/2$" fabric blocks together to make one $2^1/2$" x $3^1/2$" fabric block and sew to top edge of stocking front. Repeat for stocking back.

4. Trace heart, star, and stocking heel from page 120 onto fusible web.

5. Apply fusible web with traced patterns onto back sides of fabric scraps and cut out designs.

6. Remove backing from fusible web and adhere designs onto stocking front as shown in photograph on page 70.

7. Using two strands of embroidery floss, outline designs. Use decorative stitches as desired.

8. Fold top edges of stocking front and stocking back to wrong side's seam line. Leaving an opening at the top, finish stocking by machine-stitching stocking front to stocking back with right sides together. Turn right side out.

9. Using pearl cotton, stitch through top back corner of stocking and knot to make a loop for hanging.

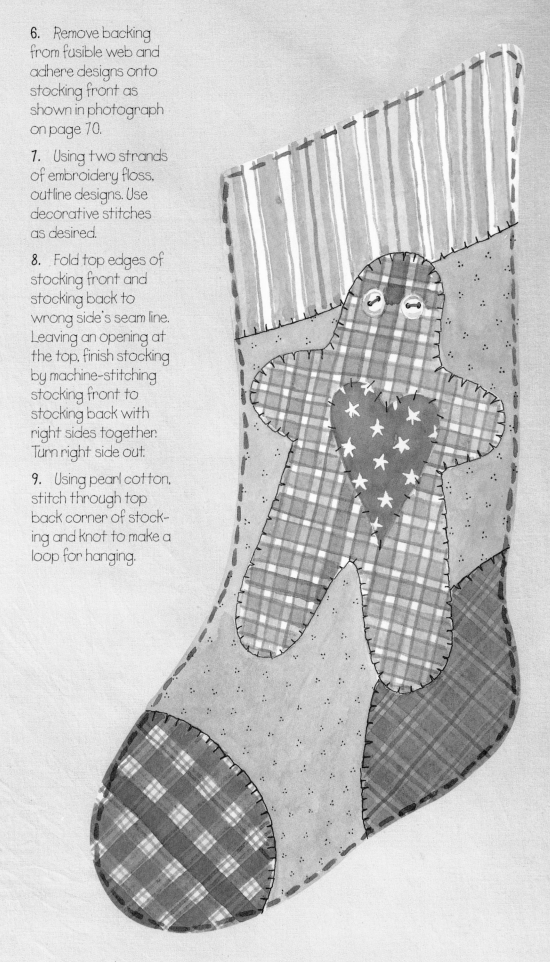

PATCHWORK CHRISTMAS QUILT

Materials:

Fusible web
Coordinating
  fabric scraps
Muslin blocks,
  a,b,c,d,e,f,g,h:
  $4^1/_2$" square (8)
Coordinating
  fabric blocks,
  j,k,m,n:
  $2^1/_2$" square (32)
Backing fabric,
  $16^1/_2$" square
Cotton batting,
  $16^1/_2$" square
Embroidery floss,
  coordinating
  color(s)

Assembly:

1. Before beginning, carefully read General Instructions on pages 10-22.

2. Machine-stitch $2^1/_2$" square fabric blocks together to make eight pieced $4^1/_2$" square fabric blocks.

3. Machine-stitch pieced $4^1/_2$" square fabric blocks and muslin blocks together, as shown in diagram, to make quilt front.

4. Trace snowman, snowman's arms and scarf, gingerbread man, heart, and five stars from page 107 onto fusible web.

5. Apply fusible web with traced patterns onto back sides of fabric scraps and cut out designs.

6. Remove backing from fusible web and adhere designs onto quilt front as shown in photograph on page 72.

7. Place embellished quilt front on top of cotton batting. Using two strands of embroidery floss, outline designs, stitching through both layers. Use decorative stitches as desired.

8. Using two strands of embroidery floss, stitch the snowman's buttons using cross stitches. Stitch eyes and mouths on snowman and gingerbread man using French knots. Stitch nose on snowman using satin stitches.

9. Leaving an opening for turning, finish quilt by machine-stitching backing fabric to quilt front with right sides together. Turn right side out.

10. Using two strands of embroidery floss, whip-stitch opening closed.

11. Quilt through pieced $4^1/_2$" square fabric blocks, by machine or by hand, through all layers.

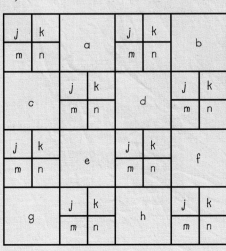

Patchwork
Christmas
Quilt
Diagram

wrap Yourself up
in the warmth of the season.

BE WARM SNOWMAN PILLOW ORNAMENT

Materials:

Fusible web
Coordinating fabric scraps
Tea-dyed muslin, 6" square (2)
Polyester stuffing
Embroidery floss, coordinating color(s)
Button
Pearl cotton
Fade-away pen
Craft glue
Seam ripper
Twigs

Assembly:

1. Before beginning, carefully read General Instructions on pages 10-22.

2. Trace snowman from page 119 onto one tea-dyed muslin square.

3. Trace heart from page 119 onto fusible web.

4. Apply fusible web with traced pattern onto back side of fabric scrap and cut out design.

5. Remove backing from fusible web and adhere design onto snowman front as shown in photograph on page 74.

6. Using two strands of embroidery floss, outline design. Use decorative stitches as desired.

7. Using a fade-away pen, trace words "be warm" from page 119 onto pillow front.

8. Using three strands of embroidery floss, stitch the words "be warm."

9. Using two strands of embroidery floss, stitch eyes and mouth on snowman using French Knots. Stitch nose on snowman using satin stitches.

10. Using two strands of embroidery floss, attach button to heart as shown in photograph.

11. With right sides of muslin squares together, and leaving an opening for turning, finish snowman by machine-stitching along traced lines.

12. Trim seam allowance back to 1/8" and clip corners. Turn right side out and stuff snowman with polyester stuffing.

13. Using two strands of embroidery floss, whip-stitch opening closed.

14. Using a seam ripper, unpick a few stitches at each side of snowman. Insert twigs to make snowman's arms and, using craft glue, secure in place.

15. Tie a fabric scrap around snowman's neck to make snowman's scarf.

16. Using pearl cotton, stitch through top of ornament and knot to make a loop for hanging.

75

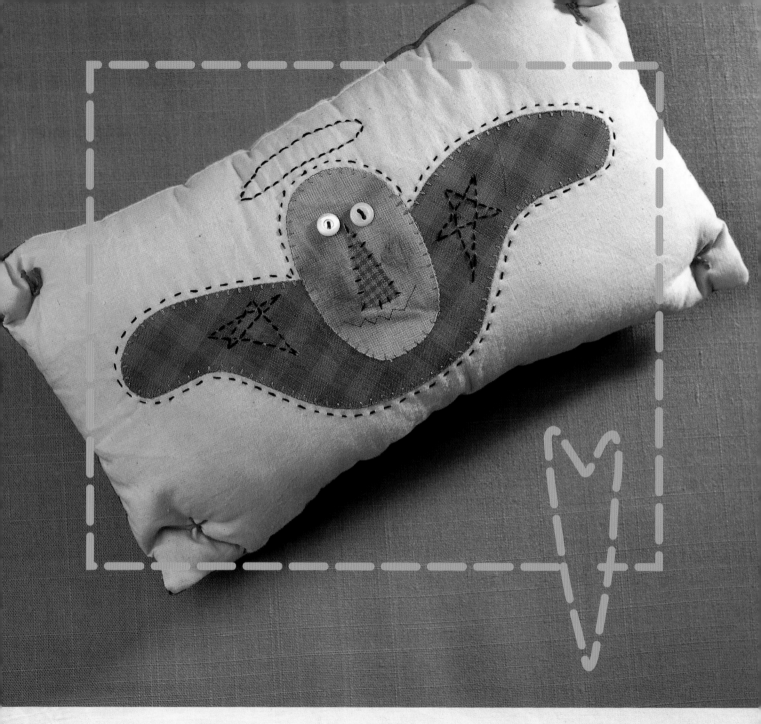

angels occupy
the lovliest corners
of our thoughts.

RAGGEDY ANGEL PILLOW

Materials:

Fusible web
Coordinating
    fabric scraps
Tea-dyed muslin,
    8" x 13"
Backing fabric,
    8" x 13"
Cotton batting,
    8" x 13"
Polyester stuffing
Embroidery floss,
    coordinating
    color(s)
Mismatched
    buttons (2)
Pearl cotton
Fade-away pen
Fine-point
    permanent
    marker
Acrylic paint, red
Cosmetic sponge

Assembly:

1. Before beginning, carefully read General Instructions on pages 10-22.

2. Trace angel's head, nose, and wings from page 117 onto fusible web.

3. Apply fusible web with traced patterns onto back sides of fabric scraps and cut out designs.

4. Remove backing from fusible web and adhere designs onto pillow front as shown in photograph on page 76.

5. Using a fade-away pen, trace halo, mouth, and stars from page 117 onto pillow front.

6. Using a fine-point permanent marker, draw the mouth.

7. Using three strands of embroidery floss, stitch the halo and stars.

8. Using two strands of embroidery floss, attach buttons to make angel's eyes.

9. Place embellished pillow front on top of cotton batting. Using two strands of embroidery floss, outline designs, stitching through both layers. Use decorative stitches as desired.

10. Leaving an opening for turning, finish pillow by machine-stitching backing fabric to quilted pillow front with right sides together.

11. Turn right side out and stuff pillow with polyester stuffing.

12. Using two strands of embroidery floss, whip-stitch opening closed.

13. Using pearl cotton, tie corners, stitching through all layers.

14. Using red acrylic paint and a cosmetic sponge, lightly add "blush" to angel's cheeks.

wise men
still seek him.

PEACE ON EARTH PILLOW

Materials:

Coordinating fabric borders,
a,b: $1\frac{1}{4}$" x $9\frac{1}{2}$" (2)
c,d: $1\frac{1}{4}$" x 5" (2)

Coordinating fabric blocks,
e: $2\frac{3}{8}$" square (2)
f: $2\frac{3}{8}$" square (2)
g: 1" x 2" (1)
h: $1\frac{1}{2}$" x 2" (1)
j: $1\frac{1}{4}$" x $7\frac{1}{4}$" (1)
k: $2\frac{3}{4}$" x $1\frac{1}{4}$" (1)
m: 2" x $6\frac{1}{2}$" (1)
n: $3\frac{1}{2}$" x $1\frac{1}{4}$" (1)
p: $1\frac{1}{4}$" x $6\frac{1}{2}$" (1)

Backing fabric,
$6\frac{1}{2}$" x $9\frac{1}{2}$"

Cotton batting,
$6\frac{1}{2}$" x $9\frac{1}{2}$"

Polyester stuffing

Embroidery floss, coordinating color(s)

Pearl cotton

Fade-away pen

Assembly:

1. Before beginning, carefully read General Instructions on pages 10-22.

2. Cut all four $2\frac{3}{8}$" square fabric blocks in half, diagonally, to make eight fabric triangles.

3. Machine-stitch fabric triangles and remaining fabric blocks together, as shown in diagram, to make center fabric block.

4. Machine-stitch fabric borders and center fabric block together to make pillow front.

5. Using a fade-away pen, trace star and phrase from page 119 onto pillow front.

6. Place embellished pillow front on top of cotton batting. Using two strands of embroidery floss, outline fabric blocks, stitching through both layers. Use decorative stitches as desired.

7. Using three strands of embroidery floss, stitch the star and the phrase.

8. Leaving an opening for turning, finish pillow by machine-stitching backing fabric to quilted pillow front with right sides together.

9. Turn right side out and stuff pillow with polyester stuffing.

10. Using two strands of embroidery floss, whip-stitch opening closed.

11. Using pearl cotton, tie corners where fabric borders connect, stitching through all layers.

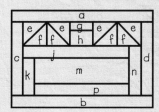

Peace on Earth Pillow Diagram

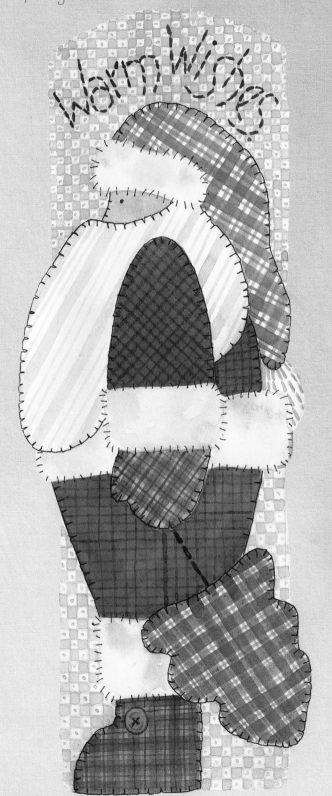

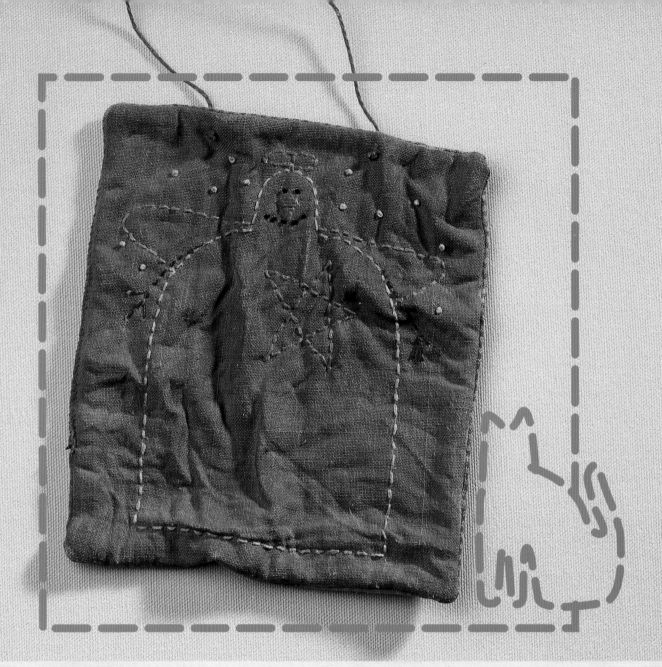

at christmas time
when angels call,
hope and peace
will come to all.

STITCHED SNOW ANGEL ORNAMENT

Materials:

Coordinating fabric block, $6\frac{1}{2}$" x 6"

Backing fabric, $6\frac{1}{2}$" x 6"

Cotton batting, $6\frac{1}{2}$" x 6"

Embroidery floss, coordinating color(s)

Pearl cotton

Fade-away pen

Fabric stiffener

Assembly:

1. Before beginning, carefully read General Instructions on pages 10-22.

2. Using a fade-away pen, trace snow angel from page 122 onto fabric block.

3. Place fabric block on top of cotton batting. Using three strands of embroidery floss, stitch design, stitching through both layers. Use decorative stitches as desired.

4. Using two strands of embroidery floss, stitch eyes and mouth on angel and snow in background using French knots. Stitch nose on angel using satin stitches.

5. Leaving an opening for turning, finish ornament by machine-stitching backing fabric to quilted ornament front with right sides together. Turn right side out.

6. Using two strands of embroidery floss, whip-stitch opening closed.

7. Using pearl cotton, stitch through top of ornament and knot in front to make a loop for hanging.

8. Using fabric stiffener, stiffen ornament following manufacturer's directions.

it is good to be
children sometimes,
and never better
than at christmastime.

- charles dickens.

MERRY CHRISTMAS PILLOW ORNAMENT

Materials:

Tea-dyed muslin,
   5" square
Backing fabric,
   5" square
Cotton batting,
   5" square
Polyester stuffing
Embroidery floss,
   coordinating
   color(s)
Pearl cotton
Fade-away pen

Assembly:

1.   Before beginning, carefully read General Instructions on pages 10-22.

2.   Using a fade-away pen, trace words "merry christmas" and border from page 119 onto tea-dyed muslin.

3.   Place tea-dyed muslin on top of cotton batting. Using three strands of embroidery floss, stitch words "merry christmas" and border, stitching through both layers. Use decorative stitches as desired.

4.   Using two strands of embroidery floss, add dot over letter "i" using a French knot.

5.   Leaving an opening for turning, finish pillow by machine-stitching backing fabric to quilted pillow front with right sides together.

6.   Turn right side out and stuff pillow with polyester stuffing.

7.   Using two strands of embroidery floss, whip-stitch opening closed.

8.   Using pearl cotton, stitch through top of ornament and knot to make a loop for hanging.

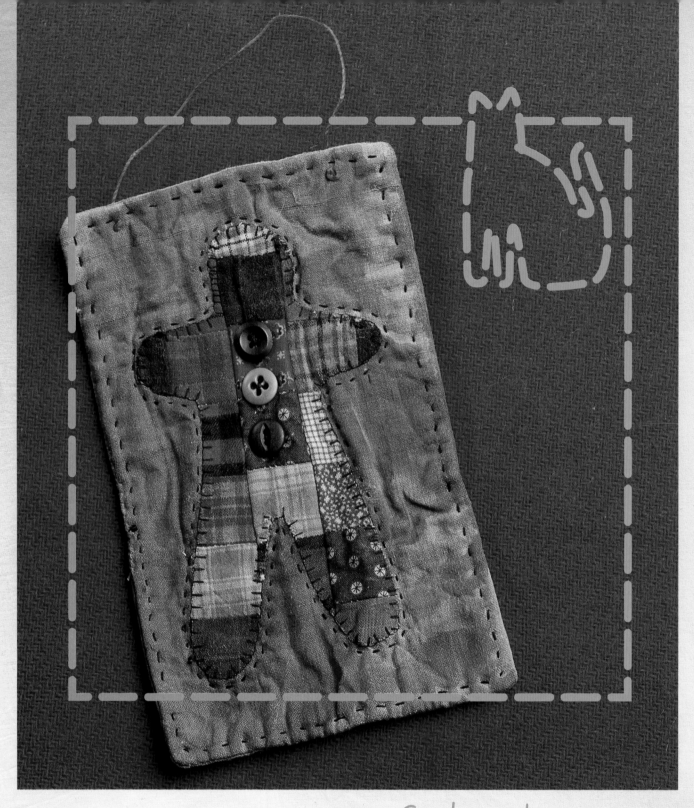

a pocket full of christmas
a season full of cheer.

PATCHWORK GINGERBREAD MAN ORNAMENT

Materials:

Fusible web
Coordinating
    fabric blocks,
    1½" square (35)
    8½" x 5½" (1)
Backing fabric,
    8½" x 5½"
Cotton batting,
    8½" x 5½"
Embroidery floss,
    coordinating
    color(s)
Mismatched
    buttons (3)
Pearl cotton
Fabric stiffener

Assembly:

1. Before beginning, carefully read General Instructions on pages 10-22.

2. Machine-stitch 1½" square fabric blocks together to make one pieced 7½" x 5½" fabric block (seven down; five across).

3. Trace gingerbread man from page 108 onto fusible web.

4. Apply fusible web with traced pattern onto back side of pieced fabric block and cut out design.

5. Remove backing from fusible web and adhere design onto 8½" x 5½" fabric block as shown in photograph on page 84.

6. Place embellished ornament front on top of cotton batting. Using three strands of embroidery floss, outline 9" x 6" fabric block and design, stitching through both layers. Use decorative stitches as desired.

7. Using two strands of embroidery floss, attach buttons to gingerbread man.

8. Leaving an opening for turning, finish ornament by machine-stitching backing fabric to quilted

9. Using two strands of embroidery floss, whip-stitch opening closed.

10. Using pearl cotton, stitch through top of ornament and knot in front to make a loop for hanging.

11. Using fabric stiffener, stiffen ornament following manufacturer's directions.

ornament front with right sides together. Turn right side out.

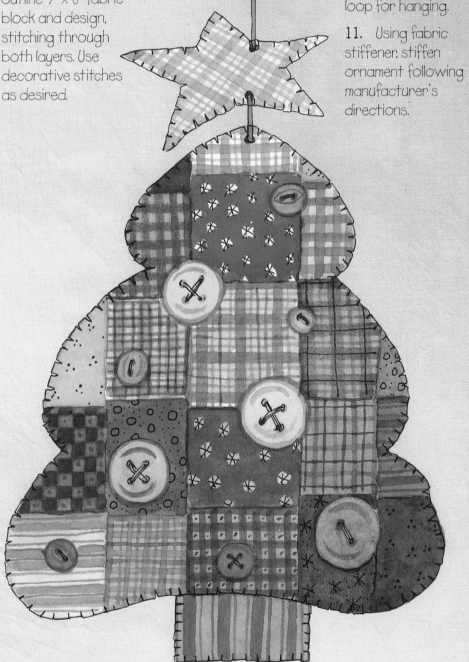

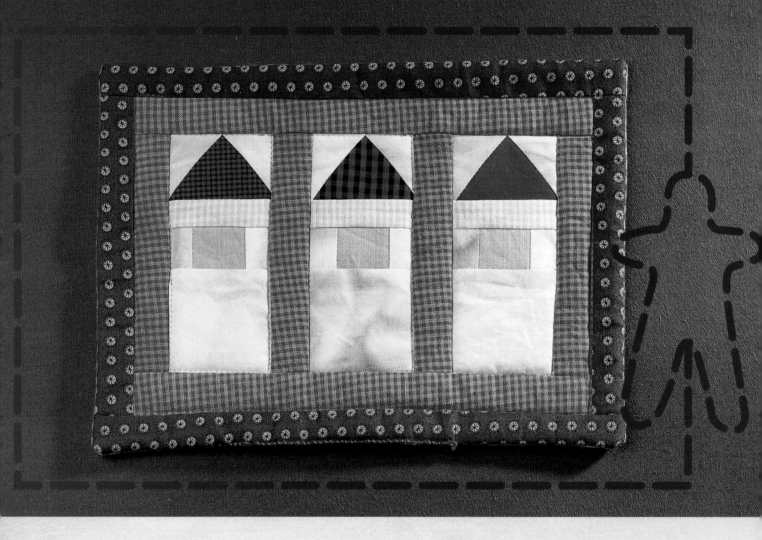

joy is not something you wish for,
it's something you make,
something you do,
something you are,
and something you give away.

PRIMITIVE SANTA QUILT

Materials:

Coordinating fabric borders,
  outer:
  a,b: 1" x 9½" (2)
  c,d: 1" x 6¼" (2)
  inner:
  e,f: 1" x 8½" (2)
  g,h,j,k: 1" x 5¼" (4)
Coordinating fabric blocks,
  m,n: 3" square (6)
  p: 1" x 2½" (3)
  q: 1¼" x 1" (6)
  r: 1¼" x 1½" (3)
  s: 2½" square (3)
Backing fabric,
  7¼" x 9½"
Cotton batting,
  7¼" x 9½"
Embroidery floss,
  coordinating
  color(s)

Assembly:

1. Before beginning, carefully read General Instructions on pages 10-22.

2. Trace large center triangle from page 125 onto three 3" square fabric blocks and cut out. Trace remaining two triangles from page 125 onto remaining three 3" square fabric blocks and cut out.

3. For each primitive Santa section, machine-stitch three fabric triangles, one 1" x 2½" fabric block, two 1¼" x 1" fabric blocks, one 1¼" x 1½" fabric block, and one 2½" x 2½" fabric block together, as shown in diagram.

4. Machine-stitch fabric borders and all three primitive Santas together to make quilt front.

5. Place pieced quilt front on top of cotton batting. Using two strands of embroidery floss, outline center fabric block, stitching through both layers. Use decorative stitches as desired.

6. Leaving an opening for turning, finish quilt by machine-stitching backing fabric to quilt front with right sides together. Turn right side out.

7. Using two strands of embroidery floss, whip-stitch opening closed.

8. Quilt by machine, or by hand, through all layers.

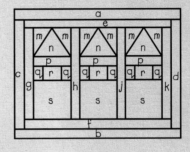

Primitive
Santa
Quilt
Diagram

SANTA STITCHERY QUILT

Materials:

Coordinating fabric borders,
a,b: 1" x 7" (2)
c,d: 1" x 9¼" (2)
Tea-dyed muslin,
8¼" x 7"
Backing fabric,
9¼" x 8"
Cotton batting,
9¼" x 8"
Embroidery floss,
coordinating
color(s)
Fade-away pen

Assembly:

1. Before beginning, carefully read General Instructions on pages 10-22.

2. Machine-stitch fabric borders and tea-dyed muslin together, as shown in diagram, to make quilt front.

3. Using a fade-away pen, trace Santa design from page 123 onto quilt front.

4. Place quilt front on top of cotton batting. Using three strands of embroidery floss, stitch Santa design, stitching through both layers. Use decorative stitches as desired.

Santa Stitchery Diagram

5. Using three strands of embroidery floss, add Santa's eye and berries using French knots.

6. Using two strands of embroidery floss, fill in star using French knots.

7. Leaving an opening for turning, finish quilt by machine-stitching backing fabric to quilt front with right sides together. Turn right side out.

8. Using two strands of embroidery floss, whip-stitch opening closed.

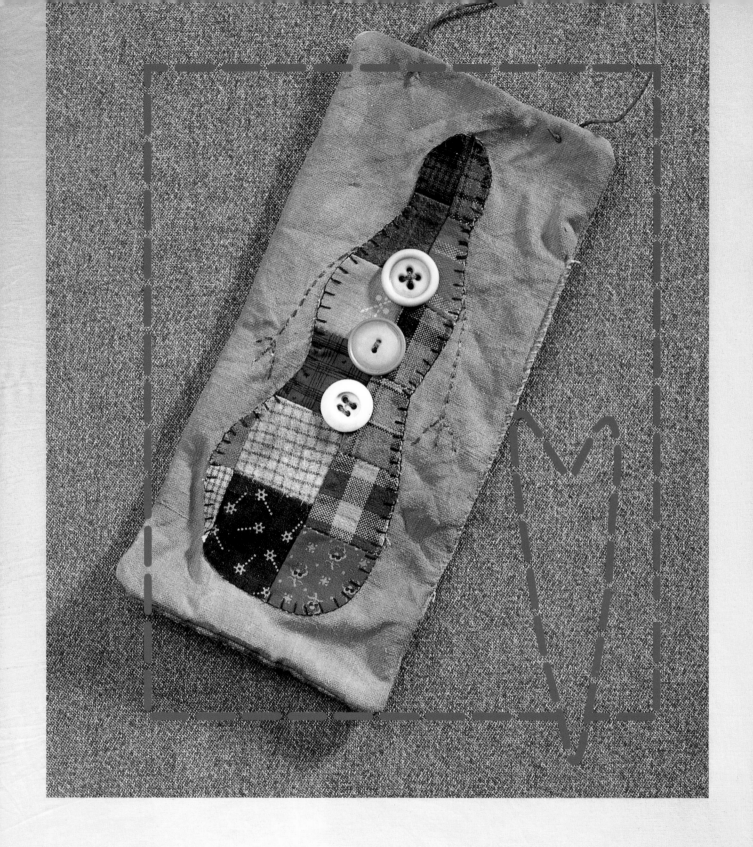

snowbody's perfect.

PATCHWORK SNOWMAN ORNAMENT

Materials:

Fusible web
Coordinating
    fabric blocks,
    $1^1/2$" square (18)
    $8^1/2$" x $4^1/2$" (1)
Backing fabric,
    $8^1/2$" x $4^1/2$"
Cotton batting,
    $8^1/2$" x $4^1/2$"
Embroidery floss,
    coordinating
    color(s)
Mismatched
    buttons (3)
Pearl cotton
Fade-away pen
Fabric stiffener

Assembly:

1. Before beginning, carefully read General Instructions on pages 10-22.

2. Machine-stitch $1^1/2$" square fabric blocks together to make one pieced $6^1/2$" x $3^1/2$" fabric block (six down; three across).

3. Trace snowman from page 125 onto fusible web.

4. Apply fusible web with traced pattern onto back side of pieced fabric block and cut out design.

5. Remove backing from fusible web and adhere design onto $8^1/2$" x $4^1/2$" fabric block as shown in photograph on page 90.

6. Using a fade-away pen, trace snowman's arms from page 125 onto ornament front.

7. Place embellished ornament front on top of cotton batting. Using three strands of embroidery floss, outline design, stitching through both layers. Use decorative stitches as desired.

8. Using three strands of embroidery floss, stitch the snowman's arms.

9. Using two strands of embroidery floss, attach buttons to snowman.

10. Leaving an opening for turning, finish ornament by machine-stitching backing fabric to quilted ornament front with right sides together. Turn right side out.

11. Using two strands of embroidery floss, whip-stitch opening closed.

12. Using pearl cotton, stitch through top of ornament and knot in front to make a loop for hanging.

13. Using fabric stiffener, stiffen ornament following manufacturer's directions.

91

PRIMITIVE ANGEL PILLOW

Materials:

Coordinating
   fabric borders,
   outer:
   a,b: $1\frac{1}{2}$" x 9" (2)
   c,d: $1\frac{1}{2}$" x $14\frac{1}{2}$" (2)
   inner:
   e,f: $1\frac{1}{2}$" x 7" (2)
   g,h: $1\frac{1}{2}$" x $12\frac{1}{2}$" (2)
Coordinating
   fabric blocks,
   j: $2\frac{1}{2}$" x 1" (2)
   k,m: $2\frac{7}{8}$" square (2)
   n: $2\frac{1}{2}$" x 2" (1)
   p: $1\frac{1}{2}$" x 1" (2)
   q: $1\frac{1}{2}$" x 6" (1)
   r: $5\frac{1}{2}$" x $2\frac{1}{4}$" (2)
   s: $5\frac{1}{2}$" x $3\frac{1}{2}$" (1)
   t: $2\frac{1}{2}$" x $3\frac{1}{4}$" (2)
   u: $2\frac{1}{2}$" x $1\frac{1}{2}$" (1)
Backing fabric,
   $14\frac{1}{2}$" x 11"
Cotton batting,
   $14\frac{1}{2}$" x 11"
Polyester stuffing
Embroidery floss,
   coordinating
   color(s)
Pearl cotton

Assembly:

1. Before beginning,
carefully read General
Instructions on
pages 10-22.

2. Cut both $2\frac{7}{8}$"
square fabric blocks in
half, diagonally, to make
four fabric triangles.

3. Machine-stitch
fabric triangles and
remaining fabric blocks
together, as shown in
diagram, to make
center fabric block.

4. Machine-stitch
fabric borders
and center fabric
block together to
make pillow front.

5. Place embellished
pillow front on top
of cotton batting.
Using two strands
of embroidery floss,
outline fabric blocks,
stitching through
both layers. Use
decorative stitches
as desired.

6. Leaving an opening
for turning, finish pillow
by machine-stitching
backing fabric to
quilted pillow front.

7. Turn right side out
and stuff pillow with
polyester stuffing.

8. Using two strands
of embroidery floss,
whip-stitch opening
closed.

with right sides
together.

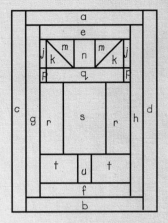

Primitive
Angel
Pillow
Diagram

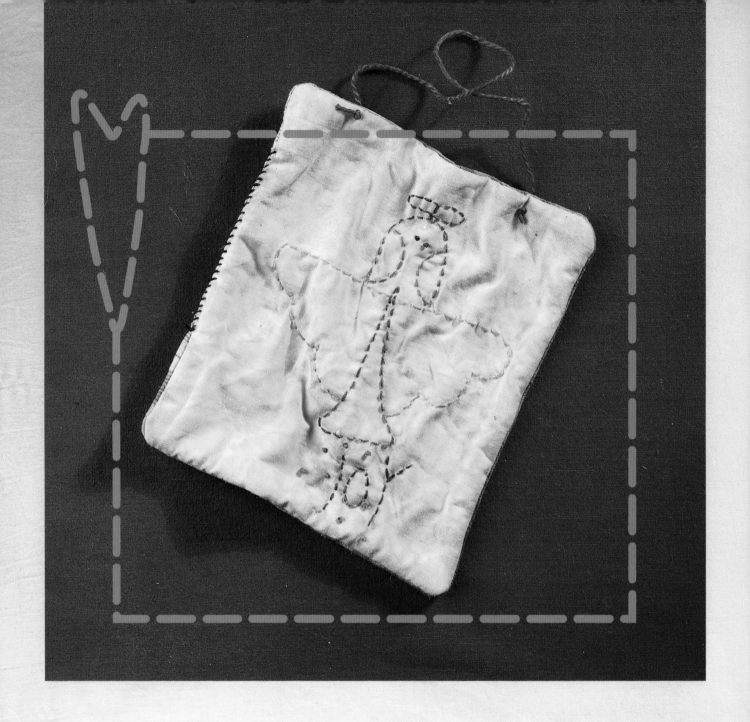

joyful hearts
hear angels Sing.

STITCHED JOY ANGEL ORNAMENT

Materials:

Tea-dyed muslin,
   6" x 5$\frac{1}{2}$"
Backing fabric,
   6" x 5$\frac{1}{2}$"
Cotton batting,
   6" x 5$\frac{1}{2}$"
Embroidery floss,
   coordinating
   color(s)
Pearl cotton
Fade-away pen
Fabric stiffener

Assembly:

1. Before beginning, carefully read General Instructions on pages 10-22.

2. Using a fade-away pen, trace joy angel and word "joy" from page 122 onto tea-dyed muslin.

3. Place tea-dyed muslin on top of cotton batting. Using three strands of embroidery floss, stitch designs, stitching through both layers. Use decorative stitches as desired.

4. Using two strands of embroidery floss, stitch eyes on angel and snow in background around the word "joy" using French knots.

5. Leaving an opening for turning, finish ornament by machine-stitching backing fabric to quilted ornament front with right sides together. Turn right side out.

6. Using two strands of embroidery floss, whip-stitch opening closed.

7. Using pearl cotton, stitch through top of ornament and knot in front to make a loop for hanging.

8. Using fabric stiffener, stiffen ornament following manufacturer's directions.

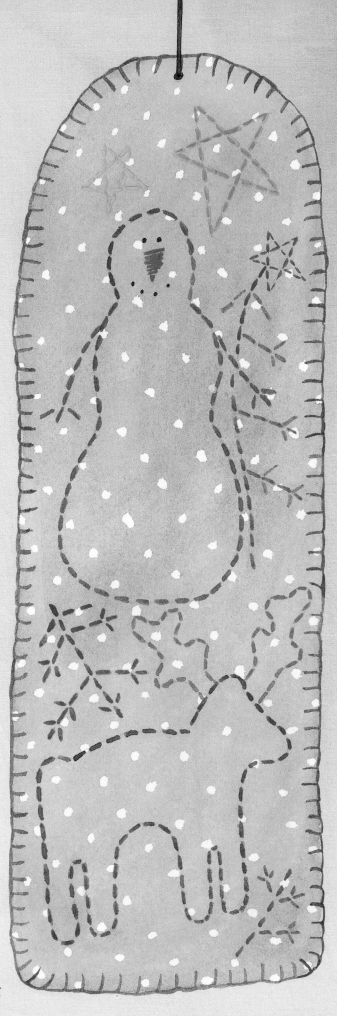

95

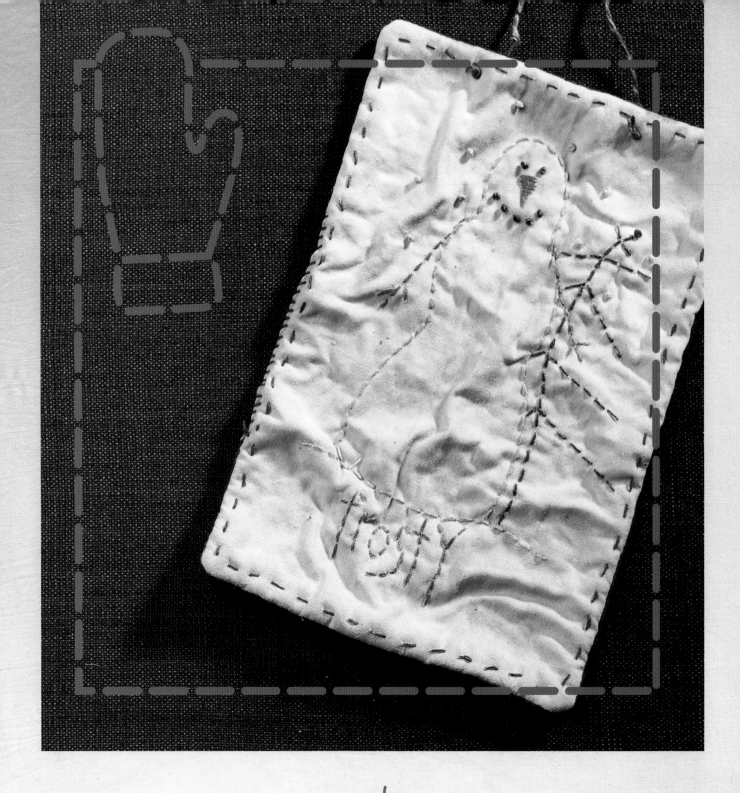

in the meadow,
you can build a snowman.

STITCHED FROSTY ORNAMENT

Materials:

Tea-dyed muslin,
   7" x 5"
Backing fabric,
   7" x 5"
Cotton batting,
   7" x 5"
Embroidery floss,
   coordinating
   color(s)
Pearl cotton
Fade-away pen
Fabric stiffener

Assembly:

1. Before beginning, carefully read General Instructions on pages 10-22.

2. Using a fade-away pen, trace snowman, tree, and word "frosty" from page 122 onto tea-dyed muslin.

3. Place tea-dyed muslin on top of cotton batting. Using three strands of embroidery floss, outline tea-dyed muslin and stitch designs, stitching through both layers. Use decorative stitches as desired.

4. Using two strands of embroidery floss, stitch eyes and mouth on snowman, snow in background, and berries on tree using French knots. Stitch nose on snowman using satin stitches.

5. Leaving an opening for turning, finish ornament by machine-stitching backing fabric to quilted ornament front with right sides together. Turn right side out.

6. Using two strands of embroidery floss, whip-stitch opening closed.

7. Using pearl cotton, stitch through top of ornament and knot in front to make a loop for hanging.

8. Using fabric stiffener, stiffen ornament following manufacturer's directions.

HOUSE IN THE WOODS QUILT

Materials:

Fusible web
Coordinating fabric scraps
Coordinating fabric border,
a: $2\frac{1}{2}$" x $16\frac{1}{2}$" (1)
Coordinating fabric blocks,
b,d: $7\frac{1}{2}$" x $3\frac{1}{2}$" (2)
c,e: $7\frac{1}{2}$" x $4\frac{1}{2}$" (2)
f: $7\frac{1}{2}$" x $2\frac{1}{2}$" (1)
g,h,j,k,m,n,p,q,r,s,t,u:
$4\frac{1}{2}$" square (12)
Backing fabric,
$21\frac{1}{2}$" x $16\frac{1}{2}$"
Cotton batting,
$21\frac{1}{2}$" x $16\frac{1}{2}$"
Embroidery floss, coordinating color(s)
Mismatched buttons (9)
Pearl cotton

Assembly:

1. Before beginning, carefully read General Instructions on pages 10-22.

2. Machine-stitch fabric border and fabric blocks together, as shown in diagram, to make quilt front.

3. Trace moon, star, house, roof, door, windows, and three trees and tree trunks from page 124 onto fusible web.

4. Apply fusible web with traced patterns onto back sides of fabric scraps and cut out designs.

5. Remove backing from fusible web and adhere designs onto quilt front as shown in photograph on page 98.

5. Place embellished quilt front on top of cotton batting. Using two strands of embroidery floss, outline designs, stitching through both layers. Use decorative stitches as desired.

6. Leaving an opening for turning, finish quilt by machine-stitching backing fabric to quilt front with right sides together. Turn right side out.

7. Using two strands of embroidery floss, whip-stitch opening closed.

8. Quilt around fabric blocks, by machine or by hand, through all layers.

9. Using pearl cotton, attach buttons as shown in photograph, stitching through all layers.

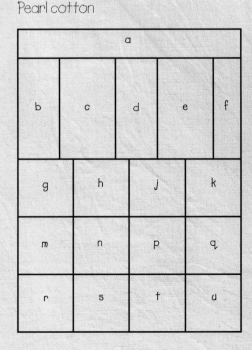

House in the Woods Quilt Diagram

make a wish.

PRIMITIVE SNOWMAN ORNAMENT

Materials:

Coordinating
    fabric borders,
    a,b: 1" x 3½" (2)
    c,d: 1" x 5½" (2)
Coordinating
    fabric blocks,
    e: 2" x 1½" (1)
    f,g: 1½" square (2)
    h: 1" x 2" (1)
    j: 1" square (1)
    k: 3" x 1¼" (2)
    m: 3" x 2" (1)
Backing fabric,
    5½" x 4½"
Cotton batting,
    5½" x 4½"
Embroidery floss,
    coordinating
    color(s)
Pearl cotton
Fabric stiffener

Assembly:

1.   Before beginning, carefully read General Instructions on pages 10-22.

2.   Machine-stitch fabric blocks together, as shown in diagram, to make center fabric block.

3.   Machine-stitch fabric borders and center fabric block together to make ornament front.

4.   Place pieced ornament front on top of cotton batting. Using three strands of embroidery floss, outline center fabric block, snowman's head and body, stitching through both layers. Use decorative stitches as desired.

5.   Leaving an opening for turning, finish ornament by machine-stitching backing fabric to quilted ornament front with right sides together. Turn right side out.

6.   Using two strands of embroidery floss, whip-stitch opening closed.

7.   Using pearl cotton, stitch through top of ornament and knot in front to make a loop for hanging.

8.   Using fabric stiffener, stiffen ornament following manufacturer's directions.

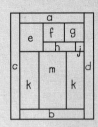

Primitive
Snowman
Ornament
Diagram

HOUSE IN THE WOODS TABLE RUNNER

Materials:

Fusible web

Coordinating fabric scraps

Coordinating fabric borders,
 a,b: $2^1/_2$" x $20^1/_2$" (2)
 c,d: $2^1/_2$" x $26^1/_2$" (2)

Coordinating fabric blocks,
 e: $2^7/_8$" square (21)
 f: $2^7/_8$" square (21)
 g: $3^1/_2$" x 2" (8)
 h: $3^1/_2$" x $1^1/_2$" (4)
 j: $1^3/_4$" x 2" (4)
 k: $1^3/_4$" x $1^1/_2$" (2)
 m: $2^1/_2$" x $4^1/_2$" (2)
 n,p,q; $1^1/_2$" square (6)
 r: $1^1/_2$" x $2^1/_2$" (2)
 s: $2^1/_2$" square (2)
 t: $4^1/_2$" x $2^1/_2$" (2)
 u: $4^1/_2$" x $1^1/_2$" (2)
 v: $3^1/_2$" x $1^1/_2$" (2)
 w: $8^1/_2$" x $16^1/_2$" (1)

Backing fabric,
 $30^1/_2$" x $20^1/_2$"

Cotton batting,
 $30^1/_2$" x $20^1/_2$"

Embroidery floss, coordinating color(s)

Assembly:

1. Before beginning, carefully read General Instructions on pages 10-22.

2. Cut forty-two $2^7/_8$" square fabric blocks in half, diagonally, to make eighty-four fabric triangles.

3. Machine-stitch fabric triangles and all fabric blocks together, as shown in diagram, to make center fabric block.

4. Machine-stitch fabric borders and center fabric block together to make table runner front.

5. Trace six stars from page 125 onto fusible web.

6. Apply fusible web with traced patterns onto back sides of fabric scraps and cut out designs.

7. Remove backing from fusible web and adhere designs onto table runner front as shown in photograph on page 102.

8. Place embellished table runner front on top of cotton batting.

9. Leaving an opening for turning, finish table runner by machine-stitching backing fabric to table runner front with right sides together. Turn right side out.

10. Using two strands of embroidery floss, whip-stitch opening closed.

11. Quilt by machine through all layers.

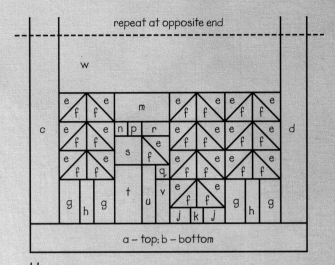

House in the Woods Table Runner Diagram

IMPORTANT NOTE

If a longer table runner is needed, the height of fabric block "w" needs to be extended. This change will affect the size of the borders "c" and "d," the backing fabric measurements, and the cotton batting measurements.

STAR
QUILT &
MEOWY
CHRISTMAS
PILLOW
PATTERNS

a meowy christmas

ANGEL
BOX &
REJOICE
QUILT
PATTERNS

JoY

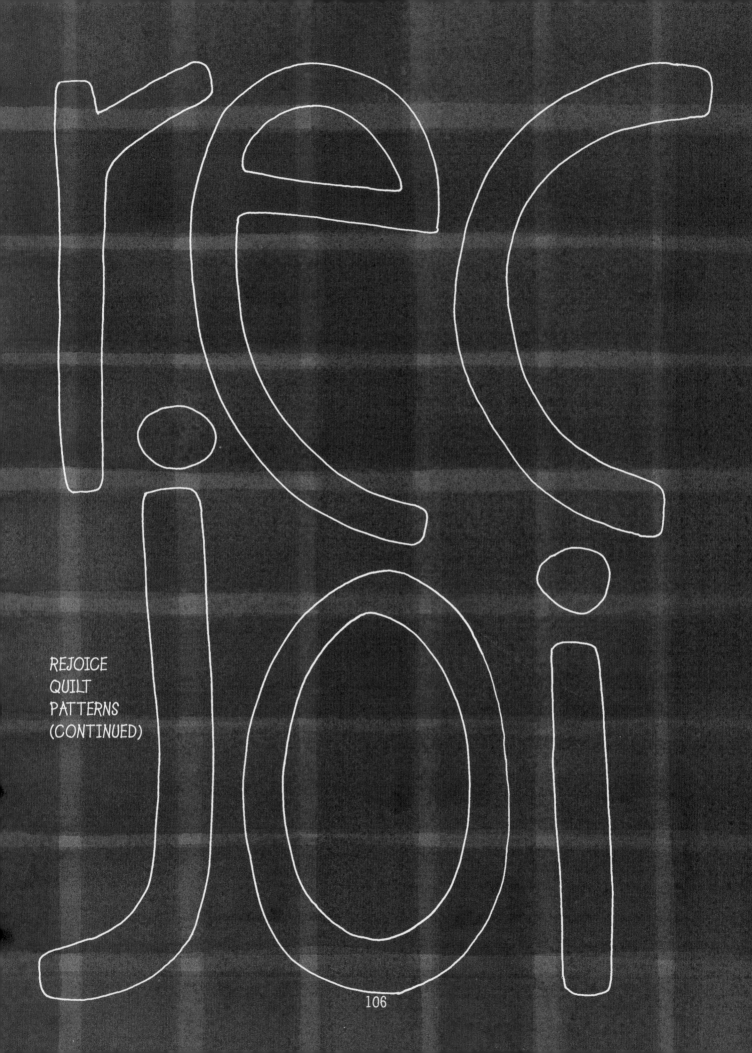

REJOICE
QUILT
PATTERNS
(CONTINUED)

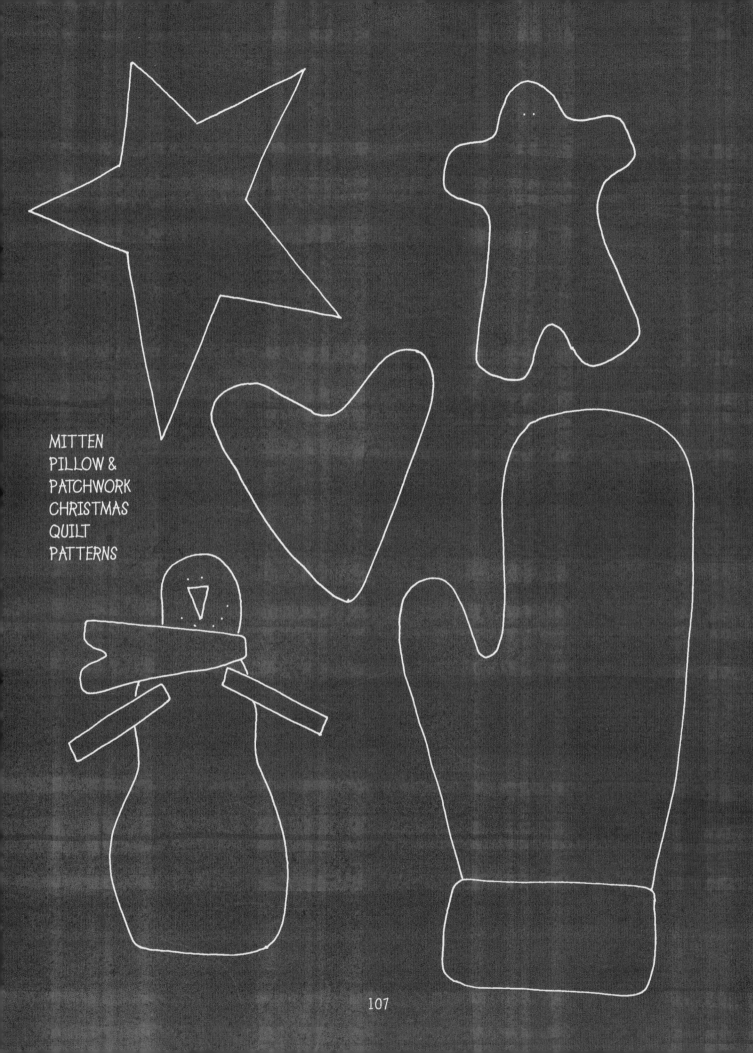

MITTEN
PILLOW &
PATCHWORK
CHRISTMAS
QUILT
PATTERNS

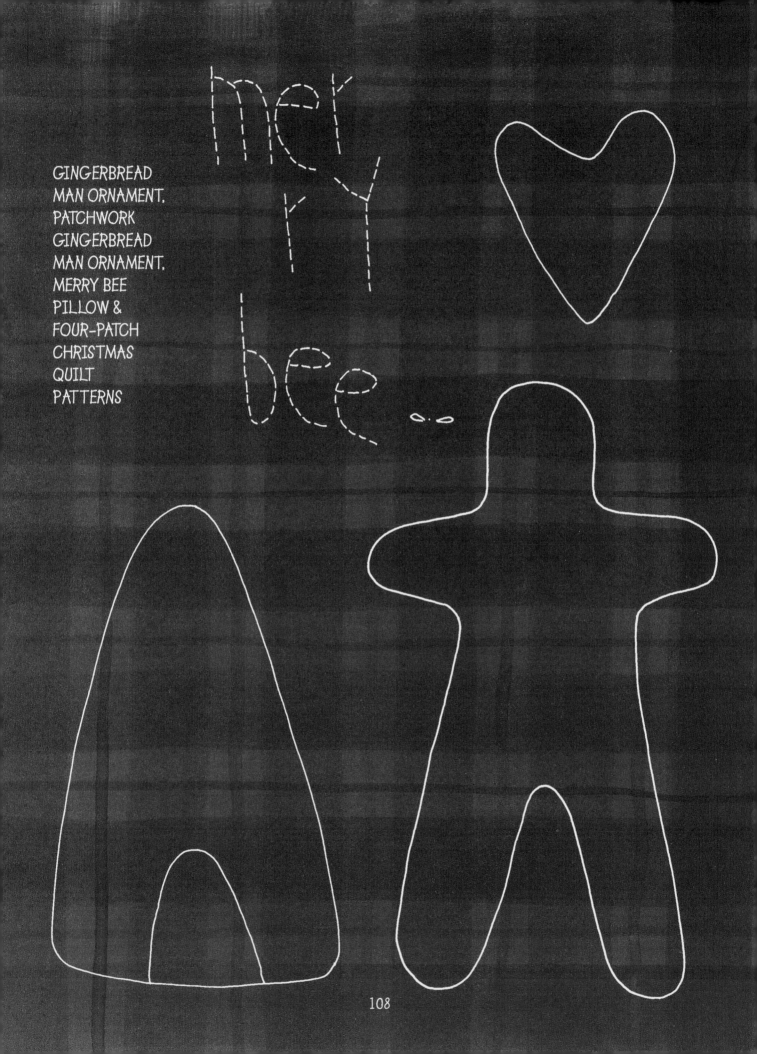

GINGERBREAD
MAN ORNAMENT,
PATCHWORK
GINGERBREAD
MAN ORNAMENT,
MERRY BEE
PILLOW &
FOUR-PATCH
CHRISTMAS
QUILT
PATTERNS

merry bee

NOEL
PILLOW
PATTERNS

STAR
PILLOW &
ANGEL
KITTY
PILLOW
PATTERNS

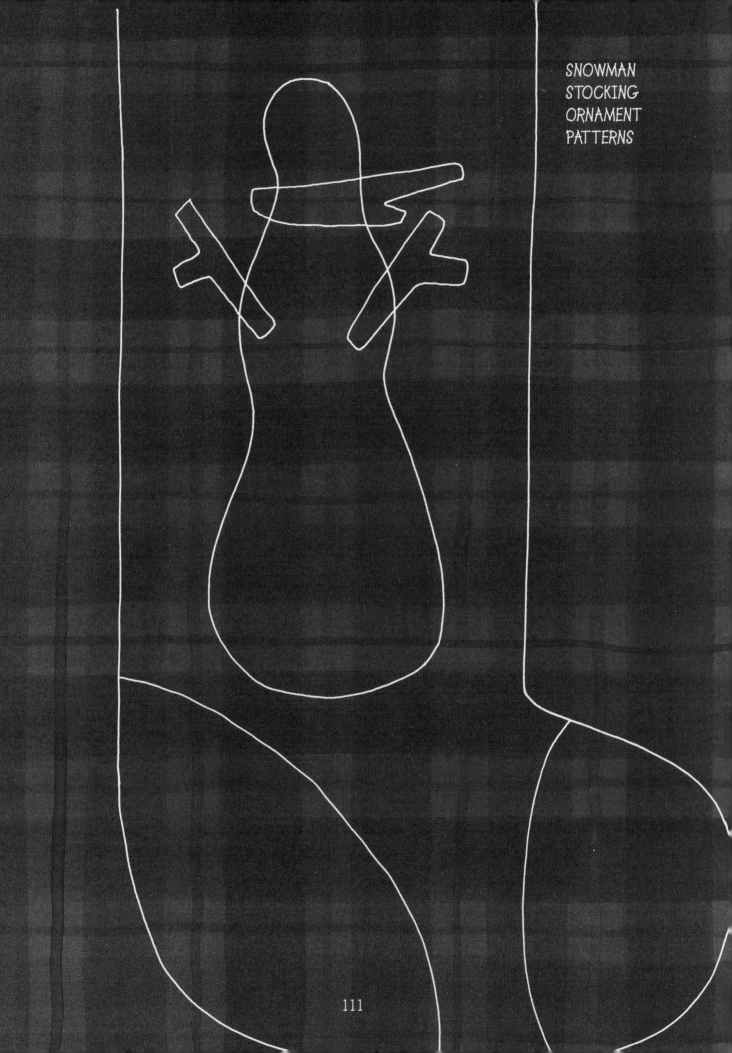

SNOWMAN
STOCKING
ORNAMENT
PATTERNS

111

KEEP
YOUR
HEART
MERRY
PILLOW
PATTERNS

CHRISTMAS
PILLOW &
CHRISTMAS
BOX
PATTERNS

FRAMED
RAGGEDY
ANGEL
PATTERNS

115

FLYING
ANGEL
PILLOW
PATTERNS

RAGGEDY
ANGEL
PILLOW
PATTERNS

RAGGEDY
SANTA
ORNAMENT
PATTERNS

BE WARM
SNOWMAN
PILLOW
ORNAMENT,
PEACE
ON EARTH
PILLOW &
MERRY
CHRISTMAS
PILLOW
ORNAMENT
PATTERNS

HEART
STOCKING
ORNAMENT
PATTERNS

FOUR-PATCH
CHRISTMAS
QUILT
PATTERNS

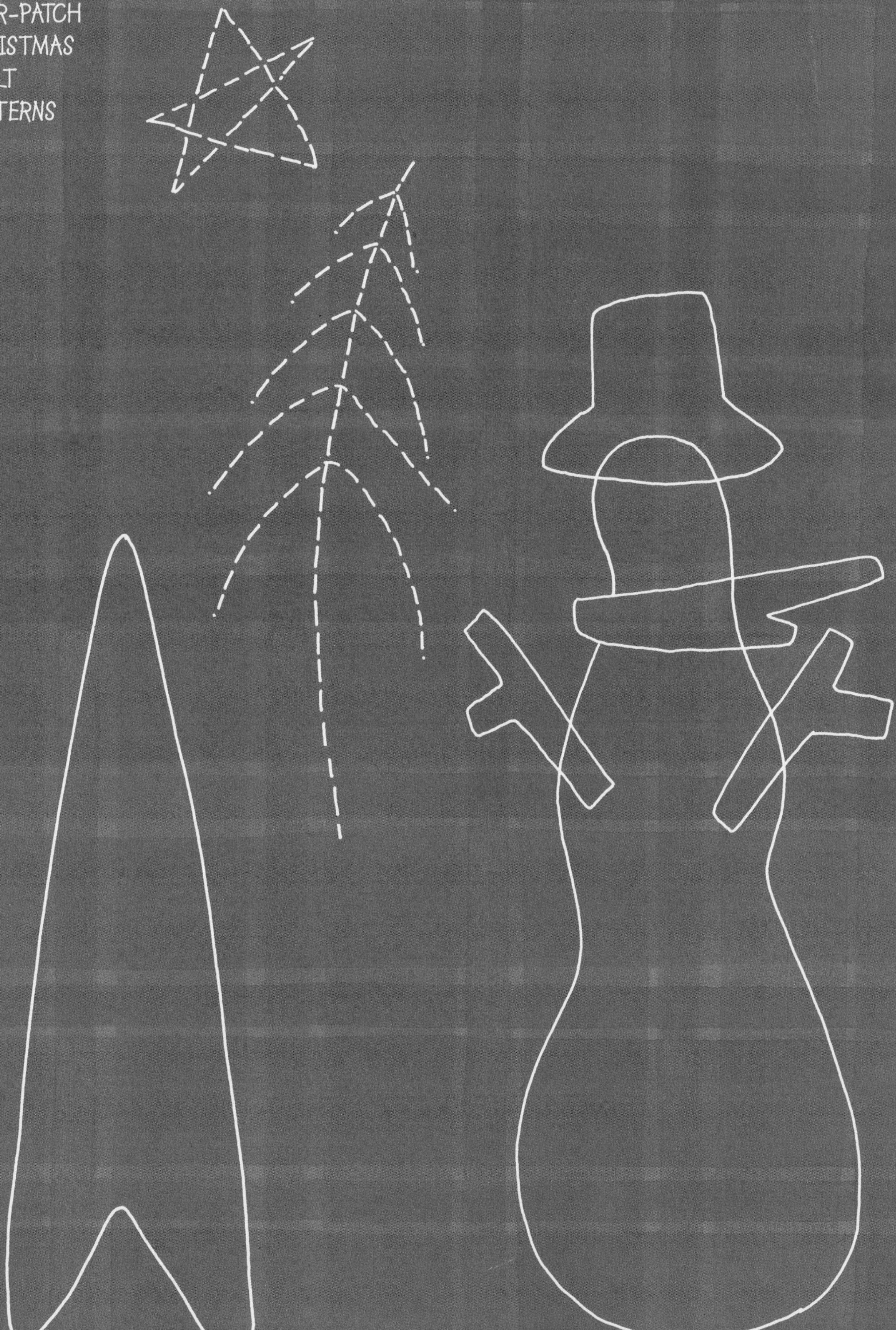

STITCHED
SNOW ANGEL
ORNAMENT,
STITCHED
JOY ANGEL
ORNAMENT &
STITCHED
FROSTY
ORNAMENT
PATTERNS

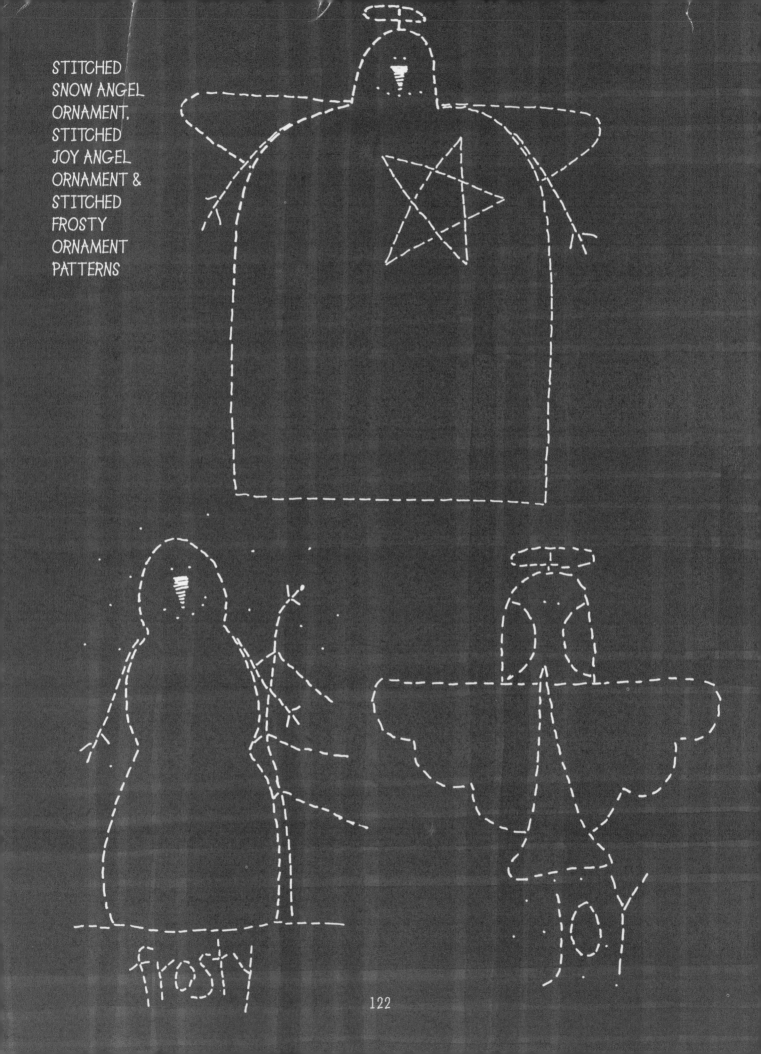

frosty

joy

122

HOUSE
IN THE
WOODS
QUILT
PATTERNS

PRIMITIVE
SANTA
ORNAMENT,
PRIMITIVE
SANTA QUILT,
PATCHWORK
SNOWMAN
ORNAMENT &
HOUSE
IN THE
WOODS
TABLE
RUNNER
PATTERNS

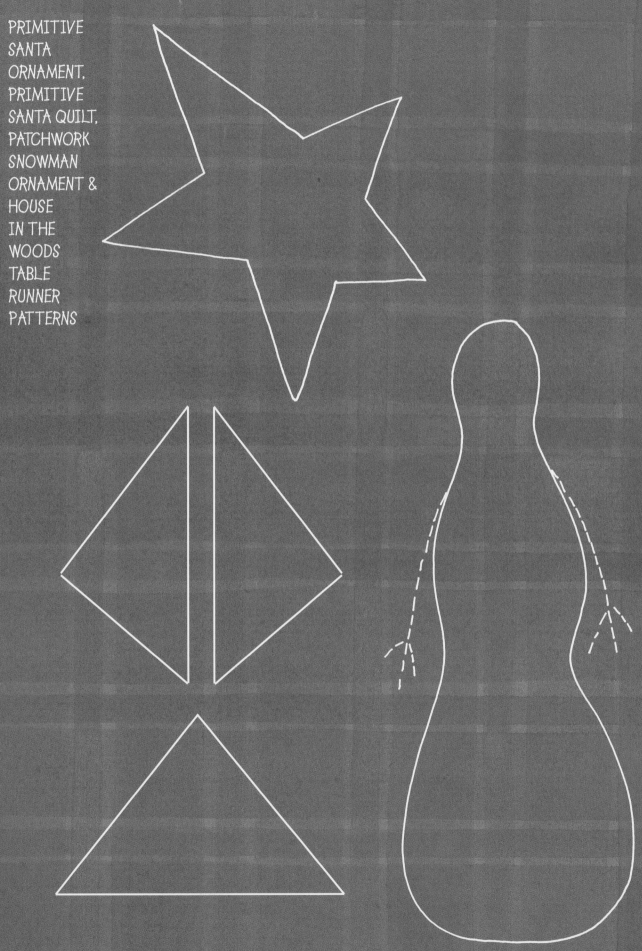

METRIC CONVERSION CHART

INCHES TO MILLIMETRES AND CENTIMETRES

INCHES	MM	CM	INCHES	CM	INCHES	CM
1/8	3	0.9	9	22.9	30	76.2
1/4	6	0.6	10	25.4	31	78.7
3/8	10	1.0	11	27.9	32	81.3
1/2	13	1.3	12	30.5	33	83.8
5/8	16	1.6	13	33.0	34	86.4
3/4	19	1.9	14	35.6	35	88.9
7/8	22	2.2	15	38.1	36	91.4
1	25	2.5	16	40.6	37	94.0
1 1/4	32	3.2	17	43.2	38	96.5
1 1/2	38	3.8	18	45.7	39	99.1
1 3/4	44	4.4	19	48.3	40	101.6
2	51	5.1	20	50.8	41	104.1
2 1/2	64	6.4	21	53.3	42	106.7
3	76	7.6	22	55.9	43	109.2
3 1/2	89	8.9	23	58.4	44	111.8
4	102	10.2	24	61.0	45	114.3
4 1/2	114	11.4	25	63.5	46	116.8
5	127	12.7	26	66.0	47	119.4
6	152	15.2	27	68.6	48	121.9
7	178	17.8	28	71.1	49	124.5
8	203	20.3	29	73.7	50	127.0

YARDS TO METRES

YARDS	METRES	YARDS	METRES	YARDS	METRES	YARDS	METRES	YARDS	METRES
1/8	0.11	2 1/8	1.94	4 1/8	3.77	6 1/8	5.60	8 1/8	7.43
1/4	0.23	2 1/4	2.06	4 1/4	3.89	6 1/4	5.72	8 1/4	7.54
3/8	0.34	2 3/8	2.17	4 3/8	4.00	6 3/8	5.83	8 3/8	7.66
1/2	0.46	2 1/2	2.29	4 1/2	4.11	6 1/2	5.94	8 1/2	7.77
5/8	0.57	2 5/8	2.40	4 5/8	4.23	6 5/8	6.06	8 5/8	7.89
3/4	0.69	2 3/4	2.51	4 3/4	4.34	6 3/4	6.17	8 3/4	8.00
7/8	0.80	2 7/8	2.63	4 7/8	4.46	6 7/8	6.29	8 7/8	8.12
1	0.91	3	2.74	5	4.57	7	6.40	9	8.23
1 1/8	1.03	3 1/8	2.86	5 1/8	4.69	7 1/8	6.52	9 1/8	8.34
1 1/4	1.14	3 1/4	2.97	5 1/4	4.80	7 1/4	6.63	9 1/4	8.46
1 3/8	1.26	3 3/8	3.09	5 3/8	4.91	7 3/8	6.74	9 3/8	8.57
1 1/2	1.37	3 1/2	3.20	5 1/2	5.03	7 1/2	6.86	9 1/2	8.69
1 5/8	1.49	3 5/8	3.31	5 5/8	5.14	7 5/8	6.97	9 5/8	8.80
1 3/4	1.60	3 3/4	3.43	5 3/4	5.26	7 3/4	7.09	9 3/4	8.92
1 7/8	1.71	3 7/8	3.54	5 7/8	5.37	7 7/8	7.20	9 7/8	9.03
2	1.83	4	3.66	6	5.49	8	7.32	10	9.14

INDEX